Shaping New Englands
**Puritan Clergymen in Seventeenth-Century England
and New England**

Twayne's United States Authors Series

Pattie Cowell, General Editor
Colorado State University

TUSAS 631

Shaping New Englands

Puritan Clergymen in Seventeenth-Century England and New England

Francis J. Bremer
Millersville University of Pennsylvania

Twayne Publishers • New York
Maxwell Macmillan Canada • Toronto
Maxwell Macmillan International • New York Oxford Singapore Sydney

Twayne's United States Authors Series No. 631

Shaping New Englands
Francis J. Bremer

Copyright © 1994 by Twayne Publishers

Twayne Publishers
Macmillan Publishing Company
866 Third Avenue
New York, New York 10022

Maxwell Macmillan Canada, Inc.
1200 Eglinton Avenue East
Suite 200
Don Mills, Ontario M3C 3N1

Library of Congress Cataloging-in-Publication Data

Bremer, Francis J.
    Shaping New Englands : Puritan clergymen in 17th century England and New England / Francis J. Bremer.
        p.   cm.—(Twayne's United States authors series ; TUSAS 631)
    Includes bibliographical references and index.
    ISBN 0-8057-4015-5
    1. Puritans—England—Clergy—History—17th century. 2. Puritans—New England—Clergy—History—17th century. 3. England—Church history—17th century. 4. New England—Church history—17th century. I. Title. II. Series.
BX9322.B74 1994
285'.9'092274—dc20   93-39232
                                                                                                      CIP

The paper used in this publication meets the minimum requirements of American National Standard for Information Sciences—Permanence of Paper for Printed Library Materials. ANSI Z3948–1984. ∞ ™

10 9 8 7 6 5 4 3 2 1 (hc)

Printed in the United States of America

For Heather

Contents

Introduction   ix

Chronology   xv

  Chapter One
Shaping New Englands: The Worlds of Puritan Clergy   1

  Chapter Two
The World of Pulpit and Print   14

  Chapter Three
Structure and Style   25

  Chapter Four
Piety   39

  Chapter Five
Polity   58

  Chapter Six
Policy   75

  Chapter Seven
Passages   89

The Clergy and Their Writings   95
Notes and References   123
Index   131

Introduction

This is a literary study by a historian. In a series dealing with U.S. authors, it examines the lives and works of men who were born, educated, and labored for a time in England. Indeed, they never thought of themselves as anything other than Englishmen. Both of these facts require some explanation.

Over the past few decades scholars in the field of colonial literature have done an extraordinary job in explicating various facets of early American writing. Norman Grabo, Everett Emerson, Sacvan Bercovitch, Pattie Cowell, Theresa Tolouse, Janice Knight, David Levin, Patricia Caldwell, David Leverenz, and others have examined the language of the Puritans in ways that have enriched the study of literature and also our understanding of the seventeenth-century world in which those authors wrote. But frequently such studies have focused on one author—as with most volumes in this series—unintentionally distorting the individual's role in the broader intellectual context. By treating the English-trained clerical authors as a group, I hope to restore some of that balance. In particular, while accepting that there were different emphases in the New England tradition, I wish to suggest that these preachers shared a greater unity in outlook than is conveyed in studies that emphasize the unique attributes of a particular figure.

Perry Miller's *The New England Mind: The Seventeenth Century* (1939) created the modern field of Puritan studies in America. But increasingly dimensions of Miller's paradigm have come under attack. And perhaps no aspect has been more criticized than Miller's assumption that the corpus of New England writings could be treated as the product of a single imagination, a single New England mind. Many scholarly reputations have been erected on the demonstration that there was no such monolithic body of thought. Diversity in belief and practice have been examined and brought to center stage, so much so that we have slipped into a quite different bog of errors. The heterodox few have at times assumed more importance than the orthodox many, and the beliefs of the region's majority have seemed threatened with neglect. Additionally, some of the attempts to highlight those who dissented from a monolithic New England mind have promoted the notion of orthodox uniformity, depicting the views of the mainstream in overly simplistic terms.

The distinction between those who built the Bible Commonwealths of New England and those, such as Anne Hutchinson, who found themselves expelled from the orthodox mansion is an important one and will be noted in these pages. But I will also seek to make the point that unity is not the same as uniformity. The orthodox mansion had many rooms. We must note the differences in emphasis and tone among the Puritan clergy of New England just as we emphasize the common perspective that bound them together and divided them from dissenters such as Hutchinson and Roger Williams.

Another goal of this study is to place the works of these men in a context that takes note of the means available for communicating ideas in the seventeenth century, the difficulties involved in print publishing, and the degree to which the presentation of ideas was shaped by the audience being addressed. David Hall has begun to investigate these matters, and I hope to build on his insights while calling attention to some additional points to be considered.

There is a real question as to whether the clergy discussed in these pages are "American"—much less "United States"—authors. All were born in England, most achieved prominence in English pulpits before migrating to America, and all considered themselves Englishmen until their deaths. Furthermore, most of their published works were printed in England primarily for the use of English audiences. As Stephen Foster has pointed out, because of the high cost of importing books, more of the English printed copies of the works of Hooker, Cotton, and others were sold and read in England than in the colonies.

There is no real question, of course, about the importance of these men to American history and literature. Yet the points made above explain in part why the focus of this study emphasizes the Anglo-American context of the story. The clergymen we are dealing with were Englishmen, thought of themselves as Englishmen, and were actively involved in the progress of English religion until their deaths. They were shaped by their English experience: John Cotton was 49 when he came to America, Thomas Hooker was 47, and though some clergymen, such as John Norton, Thomas Shepard, and Richard Mather, were younger, they too had begun their careers in England.

Chronologically, this study focuses on the period of Puritan control in New England, the years from the settlement of Massachusetts to the death of the last of the authors in the aftermath of the loss of the Bay colony's charter in 1684. Practically, the last key events discussed are the debates over the Half-Way Covenant and over the treatment of Baptists and Quakers, for by the 1670s the literary output of the immigrant clergy was exhausted. But because that period is only intelligible in the context of the English developments that produced New England Puritanism, the story begins in the Elizabethan era.

It was more difficult deciding whose lives and writings to examine. I believe that organizing a study of seventeenth-century New England along the lines of generation is a poor strategy. Those who came to New England in the period of the great migration are often labeled, logically, the "first generation." But while it may seem convenient to group them as a single generation on disembarkation, when they got on the boats in England they were recognized as belonging to different generations! Is Richard Mather's son Nathaniel a member (along with his father) of the first generation because he was born in England, and his brother Increase a member of the second because he was born in Massachusetts? How does one place John Winthrop and his son John Winthrop, Jr., both obviously leaders of the settlements in the 1630s? I have therefore tried to avoid the notion of generation and have chosen to focus on the clergymen who were trained for the ministry in England and came to New England prior to 1640. There is a considerable age spread in this group—44 years separated Nathaniel Ward and Benjamin Woodbridge, and Thomas Shepard was 20 years younger than John Cotton—but their shared experience in England in the early seventeenth century bound them together more significantly than differences in age kept them apart.

The volume is titled *Shaping New Englands* because the thrust of the Puritan movement was to transform the English-speaking world. The settlement of Massachusetts and the other colonies was in part an effort to implement the reform agenda that had been frustrated in England. But the clerical leaders of the migration also hoped that the new England would inspire and assist those who remained behind to continue the struggle to transform the old one. What distinguishes the generation of Cotton, Davenport, Hooker, and the other English-born Puritan clergy is that while they left England they never abandoned it. They were not, as Cotton put it, like Pliny's mice fleeing a house they believed to be crumbling. They retained a commitment to international Protestant reform and a belief that England had a key role to play in that change. Those who stayed in America and those colonists who returned home in the 1640s and 1650s were committed to shaping a new England as well as New England. Thus, *Shaping New Englands* is not intended to draw attention to colonial diversity but to emphasize the relevance of the colonial model for the renewal of the old England. Some may feel that I have minimized the importance of the Atlantic divide or neglected differences between New England and the mother country. Can we really read Bunyan, Milton, and Baxter for insight into the world and sensibilities of Cotton, Hooker, and Davenport? I believe that we can, and I hope that this study will generate further discussion of that perspective.

Chapter 1 develops the historical framework within which these clergymen lived and wrote, focusing on the events that gave rise to the Puritan movement, the settlement of New England, and the impact of the English Puritan Revolution of the midseventeenth century. Chapter 2 examines the means by which these clergy chose to communicate their message, not only their book publications but also their circulation of sermon notes and manuscript treatises. In chapter 3 I discuss the preferred Puritan plain style and the way in which messages were tailored to the needs of particular groups. The remainder of the volume seeks to examine the corpus of works produced by the clerical authors by dividing it into various topics. Chapter 4 examines writings that deal with theology and the details of humanity's relationship with God under the rubric of piety. The next chapter discusses views on polity, focusing on Congregationalism, which was the orthodox "New England Way." Chapter 6 uses the general theme of policy to examine Puritan writings on social matters, from the nature of the historical process to the structures of community. Finally, in chapter 7, I examine the changes of the post-Restoration era in both Englands and how the emphases of preaching and writing changed in response to these developments.

In all that I have previously written about the Puritans I have sought where possible to retain the original spelling in quotations. But in the course of preparing this study, I have rethought that practice. Addressing the issue of style, Thomas Hooker argued that clergymen should avoid "all obscure and unusual Phrases, dark Sentences and Expressions, [and] strange Languages."[1] It can be argued that for the educated reader of today the use of original spelling is itself a form of scholarly affectation that inhibits apprehension of the meaning. I have therefore decided to modernize spelling so as to lift that haze of darkness, to allow the clergymen to be heard in the language of today's audience just as they labored to compose their works in the language of the audience of their day.

Some of the research for this volume and much of the writing was done during a sabbatical stay at Wolfson College, Cambridge University. I would like to thank Millersville University for granting me that leave. I would also like to thank Dr. David Williams and the fellows of Wolfson College for inviting me to be a visiting scholar, the history faculty of the university for granting me faculty privileges, and the staff of the university library for their assistance. I deeply appreciate being named a Fulbright fellow for that period and thank Capt. John Franklin and Alison Corbett of the Fulbright Commission in London for all their help. Financial support was also forthcoming from the Academic Research Committee of Millersville University. I would like to express my thanks as well to Martin and Jane Wood, who were generous in their hospitality and who guided me through the East Anglian homeland of many of England's Puritans.

At Cambridge I profited from discussions with John Morrill, Patrick Collinson, Tom Webster, and members of the Tudor Seminar and the Seminar on Early Modern British History. My views have also been shaped by the authors whose works are mentioned herein, with many of whom I have had the privilege of discussing Puritanism. Special thanks go to Pattie Cowell, who helped to shape the original proposal for this book. Christopher Dahl, my dean and a good friend, read an early draft of the manuscript and provided much helpful advice.

Chronology

The fortunes of Puritan reform from the establishment of the Church of England to the Glorious Revolution.

1534 Act of Supremacy recognizes the king of England as the supreme head of the church in England.

1547 Death of Henry VIII. Accession of Edward VI.

1549 Publication of first Edwardian Prayer Book brings the Church of England closer to the continental Reformation.

1553 Death of Edward VI. Accession of Mary Tudor, who seeks to suppress Protestantism and return England to Roman Catholicism. The queen's policies lead to the arrest and later execution of Protestants such as John Hooper and Thomas Cranmer. Other Protestants flee to the Continent.

1558 Death of Mary Tudor. Accession of the Protestant queen Elizabeth.

1563 Convocation approves the Thirty-nine Articles, the doctrinal creed of the Anglican Church.

1567 Vestinarian controversy comes to the fore as "Puritans" who opposed prescribed ecclesiastical vestments are pressured to wear them.

1569 Thomas Cartwright begins a series of lectures at Cambridge in which he argues for a purified Christianity and presbyterian-style church governance.

1572 John Field and Thomas Wilcox publish the *First Admonition to Parliament,* which seeks to enlist parliamentary support for reform of the church.

1576 Edmund Grindal succeeds Thomas Parker as archbishop of Canterbury. Grindal relaxes pressure on reformers and clashes with Elizabeth over the value of prophesyings.

1590   Thomas Cartwright and other presbyterian leaders arrested for their activities in trying to reform the church.

1595   Archbishop John Whitgift's Lambeth Articles reassert Calvinist stance of the Church of England.

1601   William Perkins's *Treatise of the Vocations; or, Callings of men* published.

1603   Death of Elizabeth. James VI of Scotland becomes James I of England. Millenary Petition, seeking reforms in the church, presented to James I.

1604   James I meets with the Puritan leaders at the Hampton Court Conference and agrees to only minor reforms. Richard Bancroft, strong opponent of the Puritans, succeeds John Whitgift as archbishop of Canterbury.

1605   Discovery of the Gunpowder Plot to blow up Parliament fans renewed anti-Catholic sentiments.

1618   Bohemian Revolt, the start of the Thirty Years War.

1625   Formation in England of the Feofees for Impropriation, a group of clergy, merchants, and lawyers, including Richard Sibbes and John Davenport, who intend to purchase livings for Puritan clergymen. Death of James I. Accession of Charles I.

1626   Charles I prohibits predestinarian teaching at Cambridge. A similar prohibition is placed on Oxford in 1628.

1629   New England Company reorganizes and receives a royal charter as the Massachusetts Bay Company. John Winthrop and other leaders of the company sign the Cambridge Agreement, signifying their willingness to migrate to New England if they can bring the charter and powers of government with them.

1630   *The Arbella* and her sister ships sail for Massachusetts, beginning the Great Migration of Puritans to the Bay Colony. John Winthrop establishes the seat of the new colony at Boston and assumes control from John Endecott as governor of Massachusetts.

1633   John Cotton and Thomas Hooker arrive in Massachusetts. William Laud raised to archbishop of

Canterbury. Feofees for Impropriations disbanded by the courts in case pressed by Laud.

1635   Disputes between Roger Williams and the magistrates of the Bay Colony lead to Williams's banishment. Anne Hutchinson holds meetings in her home to discuss points raised in sabbath sermons. Settlers from Dorchester, Massachusetts, settle at Windsor on the Connecticut River. An advance group from Newton settles Hartford. John Winthrop, Jr., founds a settlement at Saybrook at the mouth of the Connecticut River.

1636   Massachusetts General Court authorizes establishment of Harvard College.

1637   Sermon by the Rev. John Wheelwright, a supporter of Anne Hutchinson, brings the controversy between the Hutchinsonians (Antinomians) and the orthodox to a head. Synod at Cambridge defines religious errors and attacks the beliefs of the Hutchinsonians. Henry Vane, a Hutchinsonian, defeated by John Winthrop in his bid for reelection. Anne Hutchinson and her principal followers tried by the General Court and banished. John Davenport, Theophilus Eaton, and their followers found the town of New Haven.

1639   Charles I's efforts to impose Anglican forms of worship on Scotland provoke the First Bishops War against the rebellious Presbyterians of the northern kingdom.

1640   Charles I calls a Parliament to raise funds to conduct his war against the Scots. The "Short Parliament" demands reforms and is dissolved. Second Bishops War ends with Scots granting a truce after their invasion of northern England. Charles I forced to call a new Parliament—the "Long Parliament." Root and Branch Petition presented to Parliament demands reforms of the church. Archbishop William Laud imprisoned by order of Parliament.

1641   *Bay Psalm Book* published, composed by Richard Mather, John Eliot, and Thomas Welde. Thomas Welde and Hugh Peter appointed emissaries of Massachusetts to seek English assistance for the colonies and to assist the cause of reform in England.

1642   Charles I raises his standard against Parliament. The English Civil Wars begin. Battle of Edgehill.

1643   Parliament agrees to the Solemn League and Covenant, an alliance with the church against the king and for a reform of the English church. Parliament establishes the Westminster Assembly of Divines to make recommendations to Parliament for religious reform. John Cotton, John Davenport, and Thomas Hooker decline invitations. New Englander John Phillip is among the members of the assembly.

1644   Split between Presbyterians and Congregationalists appears in the Westminster Assembly. Congregationalist minority publishes *An Apologetical Narration*. Roger Williams's *The Bloody Tenent of Persecution* and John Cotton's *The Keys of the Kingdom of Heaven* published.

1646   Book of Common Prayer abolished. Parliament enacts a Presbyterian church order.

1647   Death of Thomas Hooker.

1648   Thomas Hooker's *The Survey of the Summe of Church Discipline* published posthumously. *Cambridge Platform* promulgated, defining the New England Way. The platform endorses the Westminster Assembly's Confession of Faith and outlines a Congregational form of church order.

1649   Charles I tried and executed by Parliament. Commonwealth of England proclaimed with the government of the realm by Parliament and a Council of State. Organization in England of the Society for the Propagation of the Gospel in New England for the advancement of missionary activities among the Indians. Death of Thomas Shepard.

1652   Death of John Cotton.

1653   Oliver Cromwell dissolves the Rump of the Long Parliament and establishes the Protectorate with himself as lord protector of England.

1654   Henry Dunster steps down as president of Harvard because of his views on infant baptism. Charles Chauncy chosen to succeed him.

1656   First Quakers arrive in Massachusetts. They are arrested and banished.

1658   Savoy Conference, gathering of Congregational clergy in England, adopts *Savoy Declaration of Faith and Order,* designed to be the basis of a Congregational establishment. Death of Oliver Cromwell. Richard Cromwell becomes lord protector, recalls Long Parliament, resigns. Struggle for supremacy between Parliament and the generals begins.

1659   John Eliot's *The Christian Commonwealth* published.

1660   Convention Parliament invites Charles Stuart, son of Charles I, to assume the throne. Restoration of the monarchy with coronation of Charles II. Execution of regicides, including New England's Hugh Peter. Migration of some English Puritan leaders, especially former colonists, to New England.

1661   John Eliot's *New Testament in the Indian Tongue* published at Cambridge, Massachusetts.

1662   Cavalier Parliament passes Act of Uniformity, issues new Prayer Book in the reestablishment of Anglicanism and imposition of civil disabilities on dissenters. Synod of 1662 endorses Half-Way Covenant.

1667   John Milton's *Paradise Lost* published.

1669   John Davenport attacks the Half-Way Covenant in his *Sermon Preach'd at the Election of the Governor.*

1670   Death of John Davenport.

1675   Wampanoags under Metacomet (King Philip) attack Swansea, initiating King Philip's War in New England.

1678   John Bunyan's *Pilgrim's Progress,* Part I, published.

1679   Reforming Synod in New England adopts *Savoy Declaration* and urges a through reformation of morals in the colonies.

1684   Complaints against Massachusetts from Edward Randolph and others lead to abrogation of the Massachusetts Charter.

1685   Death of Charles II. Accession of James II.

1686   Sir Edmund Andros appointed governor of the
        Dominion of New England (Massachusetts, Maine,
        New Hampshire, Plymouth, and Rhode Island).
        Dominion eliminates popular base of former govern-
        ments.

1688   William of Orange invades England and James II flees
        abroad in England's Glorious Revolution.

1689   Rebellion in Boston topples the Dominion government.
        Sir Edmund Andros imprisoned.

Chapter 1

Shaping New Englands: The Worlds of Puritan Clergy

The clergymen who shaped what would become known as the New England Way were born in England in a period of extraordinary cultural change. They grew up amid intense conflict between the forces of the Reformation and the Counter-Reformation. They were beneficiaries of an educational revolution that had dramatically extended literacy among the middling classes and even provided many of the economically disadvantaged the chance to learn to read. They lived in the England of Shakespeare as well as Drake, of Johnson as well as Raleigh. The forces that changed England helped to fashion them and the audiences they hoped to reach.

Perhaps the most significant of all the forces shaping their world was religion. The Protestant reformation begun by Henry VIII was an incomplete one. As Thomas Hooker would later explain, the Tudor monarch had "cut off the head of Popery, but left the body of it yet within his realm!" The reign of Edward VI (1547–53) saw Archbishop Thomas Cranmer make advances in ridding the church of Catholic remnants, but those changes were reversed during the reign of Mary Tudor (1553–58), whose efforts to restore the Church of Rome included the execution of Cranmer and other "Marian martyrs" who would be immortalized by John Foxe.[1] Hundreds of other English Protestants fled to the Continent to avoid the same fate.

Protestantism as an international system continued to evolve, and those who returned from their Marian exile were well aware of the new ideas that had emerged. Indeed, they had spent their years abroad in places of refuge such as Strasbourg, Basel, Frankfurt, Zurich, and Geneva, where they mingled with the continental Reformers and saw the new ways in practice. But Queen Elizabeth (1558–1603), who restored Protestantism, was not willing to allow a further elaboration of the religious logic established by Cranmer and others in the Edwardian church. The 1559 settlement restored the essence of the church as it had been structured in 1553, but with a number of conservative modifi-

cations that were designed to assuage those still attracted to
Catholicism. The result was what one recent scholar has called "a theological cuckoo in the nest" of the English church.[2]

The Elizabethan Age would see a growing tension between those who
sought to restart the process of reform and those who resisted reform in
the service of the queen and the establishment. Reformers—soon branded Puritans—sought to dispense with liturgical vestments inherited
from Rome, to keep purging the church of symbols such as the use of
the cross in baptism, to rid the nation's churches of their remaining
icons, and to further evangelize the nation by training and inspiring a
preaching ministry. Many bishops themselves sympathized with some of
these initiatives. But the intransigence of the hierarchy as a whole led
some Reformers such as Thomas Cartwright and John Field to organize
a system of self-regulating classes within the structure of the national
church. The rooting out of this presbyterian effort in the late 1580s was
a major setback for Elizabethan Puritanism.

Without dismissing the importance of such clashes between the
Reformers and the bishops, it is important to emphasize three unifying
aspects of the religious life of the period: the emphatic and united anti-
Catholicism of the majority of Englishmen; the virtually universal commitment of the nation's Protestant clergy to a Calvinistic theology; and
the dissemination of these beliefs through oral sermons and a range of
popular printed material.

Opposition to Catholicism was one of the defining characteristics of
the Church of England during the youth of New England's founders.
The struggle between the Reformation faith and its Counter-
Reformation opponents was one in which the overt force of armies and
the covert tools of subversion were both readily employed. English
Protestants truly feared the military forces of Rome, which they frequently identified with the cause of Antichrist. Thomas Hooker was just
two years old when the Catholic king of Spain launched his armada
against the British Isles. John Cotton was but four years old when three
Catholic priests were hung, drawn, and quartered in his hometown of
Derby. Thomas Shepard was born, as he was constantly reminded, at
the "very hour wherein the Parliament should have been blown up" in
the Gunpowder Plot of 1605 concocted by Guy Fawkes and other
English Catholics.[3] One of John Wilson's earliest published works was
the long, poetic *Song of Deliverance for the Lasting Remembrance of Gods
Wonderful Works* (1626) commemorating the defeat of the Spanish
Armada and the discovery of the Gunpowder Plot. Though internation-

al religious struggles would continue to command the attention of men of faith throughout the seventeenth century, it is doubtful that the Catholic threat to England ever seemed greater than during the youth of these men.[4]

While anti-Catholicism provided one form of cement binding English Protestants together, another was their commitment to a Calvinist system of belief. Though other influences—such as the alternative Protestant views of Huldrych Zwingli and his successor as head of the Swiss Reformation, Johann Heinrich Bullinger—can be detected in the reign of Elizabeth, as they had been in Edward's, most scholars agree that Calvinism was the dominant theological force in the Elizabethan church. This is not, however, to say that England was remodeled after Geneva. The queen's views made any hope of adopting the Geneva polity a lost cause that few were willing to take up. Calvin's views on the nature of the sacraments were read but did not displace the earlier Protestant view of the Eucharist that was embedded in the Edwardian liturgy. But what English theologians did make their own was the Calvinist soteriology, or discussion of salvation, as developed by the Geneva Reformer and elaborated by disciples such as the Frenchman Théodore Bèze, known by his Latin name Theodorus Beza. Though some might differ over the subtleties, to believe in predestination was to be an orthodox member of the Church of England throughout the Elizabethan era and well into the Jacobean reign.[5]

The Reformation in England had begun as a change imposed from above by King Henry VIII, and the degree to which it was welcomed or resented by his subjects varied considerably according to local circumstances. In what was to be the spiritual nursery of New England, the southeastern regions of England—where a pre-Protestant reform movement called Lollardy had once spread—there was both considerable enthusiasm for and considerable opposition to the new faith. What made the question of popular reaction critical by the end of the sixteenth century was that for the first time many ordinary Englishmen were in a position to judge for themselves on matters of faith and doctrine. In doing so, they crossed into a new world, for as Patrick Collinson has observed:

> Culturally speaking . . . the Reformation was beyond all question a watershed of truly mountainous proportions. On the far, late medieval side of the range, the landscape consists of images, concrete symbols, mime, the ritualised acting out of religious stories and lessons, a certain artlessness.

Religion was "intensely visual." Seeing was believing, more than hearing
and much more than the privatised mental discipline of absorbing information from a written text. On this side of the divide we confront the
invisible, abstract and didactic word: primarily the word of the printed
page, on which depended the spoken words of sermon and catechism. In
crossing the range we are making a journey from a culture of orality and
image to one of print culture: from one mental and imaginative "set" to
another.[6]

And the passport that allowed one to travel to this new world across the
mountains was the ability to read.

According to Margaret Spufford, "[I]n the half-century or so after
1550 . . . the same upsurge of spending power in the countryside which
permitted the yeomanry to rebuild their houses, also permitted them to
send their sons to school and to free them from the labor force." While
this development was not uniform throughout England, the number of
schools and schoolmasters in the East Anglian region, from which so
many of the first New England clergymen came, increased dramatically—so much so that few residents of those counties could have been
beyond walking distance of a teacher. The result was an extraordinary
increase in literacy; many stayed in school to learn to write, while an
unknown yet much greater number of boys and also girls learned to read
at around the age of six or seven.[7]

Complementing this revolution, and fed by it, was an expansion of
printed matter for all audiences and at all price ranges, much of it dealing in some way with matters of religion. Tessa Watt has shown that
some of the less expensive products were illustrated in a way that signi-
fied the transfer of the imagery formerly found in churches to printed
pages brought into the home. Woodcuts portraying the devil stamping
on the Bible and similar themes reinforced the importance of Scripture,
much as in the colonies the familiar woodcut depicting Richard Mather
clutching a Bible in his hand was a means of visually empowering his
message. The textual content of many of the new cheap publications
also fostered religion. During Elizabeth's reign numerous collections of
ballads were printed, and some—like John Rhodes's *The Countrie Man's
Comfort* (1588)—contained songs that, with a Reformed religious thrust,
were designed to instruct as well as to entertain. When this genre began
to fade in popularity, it was supplanted by the "penny godly," which
likewise dispensed a general Protestant moral outlook. The official
prayer book, the psalter, and the Bible itself, more familiar to us than
this ephemeral literature, were also widely disseminated. The English-

language Geneva Bible (1560), with its strong Calvinistic commentary, went through numerous editions and was generally more popular than the so-called Bishops' Bible of 1568, though that too featured Calvinist commentary. It has been estimated that over 600,000 Bibles—and more than a million additional New Testaments and books of psalms—were printed in England before 1640, a time when the population numbered close to 5 million. Between 1549 and 1646 close to 300 different catechisms were published, some for use by clergymen, but others for the aid of godly laymen in instructing the members of their households. Published sermons, prayer books, and devotional guides proliferated as well. And in a category by itself was John Foxe's *Actes and Monuments* (1563), which was placed in all cathedrals by official order and purchased for use in the homes of countless Englishmen who were fascinated and inspired by it. The stories contained in what became known as the *Book of Martyrs* deeply shaped the self-image of English Protestantism and reinforced its anti-Catholic bias.[8]

While the seventeenth-century common laborer who read Milton's *Paradise Lost* (1667) with the aid of a dictionary may have been unusual, he was not exceptional. We must be careful not to limit our idea of the audience that existed for religious literature to those who can be demonstrated to have been able to write. Reading was typically learned at home, or from a neighbor woman, in the years before formal schooling began around age eight. There is ample evidence of the extensiveness of reading ability in England and its religious focus. John Bunyan, the son of a subsistence cottager, was sent to school to learn both reading and writing. His recollections imply that while schooling was unusual for one in his circumstances, some ability to read was not. Richard Baxter was raised in a small country town, and one of his earliest memories was of his father purchasing a work of divinity by Richard Sibbes from an itinerant peddlar. A hostile witness wrote of gatherings of the faithful in the 1580s: "[E]ager and vast crowds . . . [flocked] to perform their practices—sermons, communions and fasts." At these religious meetings, "[e]ach of them had his own Bible, and sedulously turned the pages and looked up the texts cited by the preachers, discussing the passages among themselves to see whether they had quoted them to the point, and accurately, and in harmony with their tenets" (Spufford, 33).

Intertwined with this common grasp of doctrine were elements of traditional beliefs in supernaturalism, which Keith Thomas has masterfully examined in *Religion and the Decline of Magic* (1971). This was an age in which most still believed in a personal devil and occult powers. The audiences that came to watch the plays of Shakespeare had no doubt that witches existed, nor did they question that one could be tempted to make a compact with the devil, as Faust is tempted in the play by Christopher Marlow. Certainly Protestants openly challenged the cult of the saints and many other aspects of traditional religion, yet even leading theologians shared many beliefs that later ages would decry as superstitions of the times. The more we examine the notion of "popular culture," the more apt we are to recognize that in examining England and New England in the late sixteenth and seventeenth centuries the lines between elite and popular beliefs are difficult to establish. While scientists devoted time to astrology and alchemy, laborers read *Paradise Lost!*[9]

To be raised in this world was to absorb many of its beliefs. The men who are the focus of this narrative were born to families that were comfortable if not well off. John Wilson, whose mother was the niece of Archbishop Edmund Grindal, was an exception in being born into the nation's elite. John Davenport's father was an alderman in Coventry. John Cotton's father was a lawyer in Derby. Thomas Shepard's father was a grocer. But these and the other clergymen discussed here were all able to attend grammar schools to learn to write as well as read. There are no records to reveal why they aspired to attend university, nor do we know why they embarked on ministerial careers. Some later remembered pious parents, and their schoolmasters may also have exerted a considerable influence on them. But nothing ties these English youth to what we would label Puritanism. Their families may well have seen themselves as godly people, and their zeal may have been greater than that of most of their neighbors. But there is little evidence that religious differences between Protestant Englishmen at this time divided communities as they would later threaten to do.

The Calvinistic unity of English Protestantism began to crumble in the 1610s. Clergymen in particular were forced to take sides, either to move in the new directions being pursued by many of the bishops of the realm or to stand firm on their Calvinist principles, taking the risk of being branded "Puritan" and harassed by the authorities. A layman, John Winthrop, claimed that the Puritan path became one on which "there is the least company, and . . . those which do walk openly in this way shall be despised, pointed at, hated of the world, made a byword, reviled, slandered, rebuked, made a grazing stock, called Puritans, nice fools, hypocrites, hairbrained fellows, rash, indiscreet, vainglorious, and all that is nought." Both internal and foreign affairs widened the split in the following decades, contributing to the great migration to New England and to the British civil wars of the 1640s.[10]

Perhaps the most significant cause of the change was a growing challenge to Calvinist theology, to predestination in particular. The emphasis on humanity's total reliance upon God for salvation had bred in some a sense of hopelessness. While this feeling was not a necessary outcome of Calvinist preaching and may have resulted from the message being distorted, some religious leaders began to react against it. One of the first signs of this attack had come at Cambridge, where William Barrett preached a university sermon in 1595 in which he criticized the supralapsarian doctrine of absolute predestination contained in William Perkins's *Golden Chain* (1590). But Barrett was forced to recant and was censured by the university authorities and by Archbishop John Whitgift, whose Lambeth Articles reaffirmed Calvinist doctrine. Similar challenges were brushed aside with relative ease until the 1610s. At that point anti-Calvinism assumed new importance with the publications of the Dutch theologian Jacob Arminius, who, arguing against Beza and Perkins, believed that God's grace could be resisted by men, implying some degree of free will.[11]

A new generation of bishops—Lancelot Andrewes, Richard Neile, John Cosin, and William Laud, among others— began to promote a different view of the faith. Drawing on patristic sources, they interpreted the teaching of the church in ways that allowed greater scope for free will and the possibility of redemption after falling from grace. At the same time they placed a new emphasis on liturgical ceremonies and sacramental rituals as means of grace.[12] The result was a challenge not only to Calvinism as the theological base of the Church of England but also to the English understanding of the church and its worship. Kenneth Fincham has pointed to the importance of the new emphasis the anti-Calvinists placed on "the universality of Christ's gospel through inclusive Church membership." By emphasizing the importance of prayer and worship for all parishioners, they negatively highlighted the Calvinist assertion that most were excluded from the elect chosen by God for salvation. The new ritualism also called for a richer worship properly and uniformly performed, with some of the discarded symbols of the past restored (Fincham, 231–32).

The grounds for dispute were clear, and the parties were soon arrayed. Those who stood for Calvinism—emphasizing the duties of the elect and practicing a sparse religious service centered on the preaching of the Word—were attacked as Puritans. Those who rejected the predestinarian strictness of Calvinism, who reached out to include all Englishmen in a liturgically more elaborate worship service in which the sermon was relegated to a lesser role, were labeled Arminians. The universities were among the most bitterly contested fields. Looking back at the decade of the 1610s, Thomas Goodwin—a friend and ally of Davenport, Cotton, and Hooker—recalled that at Cambridge "the noise of the Arminian controversy . . . began to be every man's talk."[13]

Many of those who later achieved prominence in the pulpits of New England were gathered together in the colleges on the Cam at that time. John Cotton had matriculated at Trinity College in 1597. He received a B.A. degree in 1602 and was shortly thereafter awarded an M.A. degree and named a fellow of Emmanuel College. Thomas Hooker (B.A., 1608) held the post of Dixie fellow at Emmanuel until 1618. John Wilson was at Emmanuel briefly in the same decade. Charles Chauncy—a future president of Harvard College—and Thomas Welde were at Trinity. Hugh Peter, Samuel Skelton, and John Wheelwright were students in the 1610s, and Thomas Shepard, John Norton, John Knowles, and John Eliot would matriculate at the end of the decade. These future New Englanders were part of a broader Cambridge Puritan network that included older clergymen, such as Richard Sibbes and John Preston, and students, such as Thomas Goodwin, William Bridge, John Marshall, Jeremiah Burroughes, and Sidrach Simpson, who would become the leaders of the English wing of the Puritan movement in the decades after the settlement of Massachusetts. A leaning toward godliness, a personal experience of God's grace, and the encouragement of like-minded fellow scholars created a network of friends who defended what they believed was the essence of the Reformed Church of England against the encroachments of Arminianism. Similar developments helped influence a smaller group of Oxford graduates, such as John Davenport, who also became identified with the Puritan movement.[14]

James I was himself considered a Calvinist, though in the latter years of his reign he gave increasing leeway to the proto-Arminians. His archbishops of Canterbury, Richard Bancroft and William Abbot, were strong Calvinists. But the king's policy focused first and foremost on the acceptance of his authority. He sought to harry from their pulpits those who openly refused to conform to the ordinances of the church. Those who occasionally conformed or were discreet in their nonconformity were generally left alone by their diocesan superiors. A number of preachers ran afoul of authority, however, when they used their pulpits to challenge the king's nonsupport of the Protestant cause in the Thirty Years War.

With the accession of Charles I in 1625 and the elevation of William Laud to archbishop of Canterbury in 1633, the crown and the church were united in support of Arminian change and the church itself was polarized between Laudians and Puritans. Both groups in the church labored to shape England to accord with their views. Efforts were made by bishops such as Richard Montagu, Richard Neile, and John Cosin to restore the "beauty of holiness"—altars were moved, icons restored, and liturgy enriched. The Reformers resisted. John Davenport played a key role in one such effort, the establishment of the Feoffees for Impropriation, a Puritan attempt to transform the church through the purchase of church livings and the induction of Calvinist preachers. Through Laud's intervention, the Feoffees was dissolved. In the 1620s and 1630s church authorities increasingly harried the Puritans, many of whom were deprived of their livings. Many made what compromises were necessary to remain in England. Others migrated to the Netherlands, but Laud and his supporters worked hard to root them out of that refuge. Still others journeyed to New England.

The settlement of Bible Commonwealths was intended not only to pre-serve the immigrants' freedom to worship God as they pleased but also to inspire those left behind. This aim was in contrast to that of the Plimoth Plantation, established in 1620 by Separatists who had sought their own religious freedom with no expectation that they would influ-ence others. John Winthrop's vision of a "city upon a hill" shaped Massachusetts, and similar hopes underlay the movement of Thomas Hooker's flock to Connecticut and the foundation of the New Haven colony by John Davenport and his followers. While some scholars have gone too far in representing New England settlers as believing they were the only hope for the transformation of England into the Elect Nation, it is clear that these colonists did see themselves as being on an errand. The chosen people of this Puritan exodus were to shape a new England on the shores of Massachusetts Bay, a new England that by its example and prayer would transform old England. It is this self-perception that explains why so much of the literary production of the founding genera-tion was directed to an English audience and English concerns. It also explains the intense interest the colonists maintained in English affairs, as well as the return of many of them, such as Hugh Peter, William

Hooke, and Thomas Welde, to personally aid the reform of the mother country in the 1640s and 1650s.[15]

Matthew 5:14 proclaims: "You are the light of the world. A city that is set on a hill cannot be hid." The two images—that of a light and that of a city on a hill—were commonly used by Puritans to discuss the requirement that the elect lead exemplary lives. The images were applied to communities: Colchester during Elizabeth's reign, Lincolnshire's Boston under John Cotton, and the Reformed community in the Netherlands at Arnhem during the ministry of Thomas Goodwin and Philip Nye, were each referred to as a city on a hill and as a candlestick with shining light. Individuals—including the Marian martyrs, William Perkins, and John Cotton—were referred to as shining lights. These images were appropriated by numerous New Englanders besides Winthrop. With typical hyperbole, Edward Johnson referred to the colonists as "lights upon a Hill more obvious than the highest mountain in the World." Peter Bulkeley employed the image of New England as a "candlestick," John Norton spoke of "a light upon a hill," and John Davenport spoke of the region and its clergy as "the golden Candlesticks and the bright and shining Lights in them."[16] They were not making the claim for colonial uniqueness that has wrongly been seen as the root of American exceptionalism. They were calling attention to the duty of each member of the elect—and even more of a community of saints such as in New England—to provide a saving example to all.

As they sought to shape their model society, the leaders of New England enjoyed a freedom from constraint that went far beyond what they had encountered in England or in exile in the Netherlands. There were no authorities to seek accommodation with and no Christian neighbors of differing views who needed to be placated. In England the Puritans had accepted much that, while not mandated in Scripture, was nonetheless not condemned. In the free air of the New World, they could start from scratch. Simple clapboard meetinghouses replaced the soaring cathedrals and small Norman churches of the English countryside. Candles, statues, and other church ornamentation were done away with, as were fixed religious holidays, including Christmas. Musical instruments were not heard within the meetinghouses, and the liturgical formulas of the *Book of Common Prayer* were discarded. Maypoles and Sabbath frivolity could be more successfully banned not only from church grounds but throughout the society. The framework of religious observances was thus totally transformed, marking visually the liturgical distance traveled by those who crossed the Atlantic.

What was true of the symbols of worship was true also of the organization of the churches, as New England clergymen shaped relatively new forms of polity and worship. The trust in their fellow saints that had sustained the Puritan movement for decades produced a confidence in congregational forms of governance in which the elect of each local church chose their own ministers and decided upon their own practices. Though it is possible to detect minor differences between John Cotton's Massachusetts, Thomas Hooker's Connecticut, and John Davenport's New Haven colony, the straining toward consensus among saints that made Congregationalism succeed on the level of the individual congregation created a regional uniformity that became known as the New England Way. Dissenters from the system existed—most notably, Roger Williams and Anne Hutchinson—but their support was limited and their challenges controlled.

Seeking to carry forth their reform mission, the colonial clergy corresponded with Puritan friends in the Netherlands and in England, responding to criticisms of the New England Way and urging the consideration back home of the Congregational practices they had adopted. They also offered prayers for the reform of the mother country, especially on days of fasting. New Englanders followed the struggles of Reformed Protestantism on the Continent and appointed days of thanksgiving for the successes of the Protestant forces of Gustavus Adolphus during the Thirty Years War. The outbreak of the First Bishops War between Charles I and the Scots in 1639 was greeted with concern—but hope soon followed as it appeared that the Puritan Revolution, which might bring triumph to the cause of reform at home, had begun.[17]

The era of the Puritan Revolution and the rule of Oliver Cromwell marked the high-water mark of Puritan efforts to shape England anew. Not all Puritans had left for American or Dutch refuge. In England itself the tensions arising from the conflict between the embattled Reformers and the Caroline church establishment served to sharpen fears of growing Catholic influence and raise concerns about the constitutional implications of the "Personal Rule" whereby Charles I sought to govern without Parliament. Religion thus contributed to the outbreak of the civil struggles of the 1640s that toppled not only King Charles but the Laudian church. The execution of the king in 1649 was followed by the constitutional experiments of the Commonwealth and the Protectorate, both featuring rule by the Puritan saints. The decade of war had also witnessed, however, the division of the saints into quarreling factions; a hard-fought struggle ensued between those who wished to impose presbyterian forms and those, including Congregationalists, who sought independence from any such establishment. The focus had shifted from the drive to reform the church to a dispute over the details of such reform. In the confusion of civil war, all sorts of mechanic preachers and religious radicals were free to spread their ideas until, in the 1650s, Oliver Cromwell, as lord protector, sought to bring Congregationalists, Presbyterians, and Particular Baptists together in an effort to impose Calvinist orthodoxy. But this attempt, and the entire Puritan experiment in England, was swept away in the aftermath of Cromwell's death in 1658.

During the 1640s and 1650s New England's clergy labored and wrote not only to influence their own society but to steer the course of English history. Some, like Cotton, Hooker, and Davenport, remained in New England but wrote privately and publicly to promote the cause of English Congregationalism. Others, both established clergymen like Hugh Peter and new Harvard graduates such as the three Mather brothers, journeyed to England to take a more direct role in the transformation of the nation and of individual congregations. For all these men the events of the period—and particularly the clash between Congregational and Presbyterian polities, the rise of the sects, and the advance of tolerationist views—raised new issues to be discussed and written about, both for domestic and English benefit.

The Restoration brought a new challenge. Puritans in England were cast into dissent, excluded from the national church and placed under severe penal restrictions. Some, including many former colonists such as Increase Mather, journeyed to the safer haven of New England. But they traveled to a refuge that was only marginally safer. New Englanders in the aftermath of the Restoration faced growing pressures from a hostile royal government that would eventually produce the Dominion of New England. Internal crises also troubled the American Puritans as parts of their ecclesiastical structure showed flaws and as the clergy were confronted with rising tides of sectarianism and secularism. Making the New England response more difficult were the deaths of many of the colonial clerical leaders before the dimensions of Puritanism's English failure were clear. John Cotton died in 1652, Thomas Hooker in 1647, Thomas Shepard in 1649, Nathaniel Rogers in 1655, Peter Bulkeley in 1659, Samuel Stone and John Norton in 1663. Hugh Peter was executed as a regicide as the Puritan regime of the 1650s collapsed and the Stuart monarchy was restored in 1660.

In their own way, the challenges to Anglo-American Puritanism of the 1660s and 1670s were every bit as difficult for the generation of John Davenport as had been the trials of the Laudian era. English nonconformists were faced with the post-Restoration Clarendon Codes. Their meetings were restricted, their political rights abridged, and their children excluded from the universities. Across the dissenting religious spectrum, clergymen found themselves imprisoned for trying to carry out their ministry. In the colonies different challenges emerged. Sectarian incursions could no longer be prevented. Prosperity brought fashions and luxuries that many regarded as excessive. The autonomy of colonial governments was challenged by royal commissioners, and the safety of the settlements threatened by Indian war. On both sides of the Atlantic Puritans had to redefine their purpose.

Puritanism was a movement that constantly faced new challenges and constantly evolved in dealing with them. To focus on the early New England clergy is to focus not on Puritanism in a definitive sense but on a particularly important period in the evolution of the movement. Faced with numerous challenges, John Davenport and his contemporaries struggled to see the light and to witness to it. The community of clergymen included the sons of ministers and the sons of laborers. It included those who had sought earnestly to conform and managed to do so for many years, but it also included young men who found themselves in trouble with the bishops almost from the time of their graduation. Diverse as they may have been, however, they shared a commitment to Calvinist orthodoxy, an evangelical piety, and a commitment to reforming society and the individuals it comprised.

Over 30 Puritan clerical authors came to America in the Great Migration, representing a substantial portion of the total ministerial migration. Some of them were products of the Elizabethan Age who had begun their ministries when the great Gloriana was on her throne. Others were but recently graduated from the universities when they cast their fortunes with John Winthrop's dream. University graduates, friends, and coworkers, these men and their colleagues were all in a fundamental sense evangelicals. They were dedicated to the salvation of souls and the advancement of God's kingdom. To achieve these goals, they relied heavily on the spoken and the written word. By looking at their means of communicating, we can gain considerable insight into the men, their beliefs, and the movement they helped to shape.

Chapter 2
The World of Pulpit and Print

The leadership of the Puritan effort to reform England rested primarily on the shoulders of the clergy. Their task as they viewed it was to reform the broader society, evangelize the nonreprobate ignorant, and sustain the faith of the regenerate. And in the eyes of the believers, this work required special qualifications. First and foremost, the Puritan preacher must himself have experienced saving grace. As Thomas Hooker expressed it, "No Minister can convert another, who hath not stood in Gods counsel, that hath not been sent by him." The ministry was an empowerment from God. Surviving diaries set forth the struggles of young aspirants to be sure that they truly had a calling and the sense of responsibility that they felt when they took up the labor. Scholars have frequently underestimated the element of religious enthusiasm that was at the heart of the Puritan crusade, misled in part by focusing on Puritan warnings against *unrestrained* enthusiasm. But it is clear that, for the Puritan, without the enlightenment that came from grace it would have been as hopeless for the minister to discern the true light of Scripture as it would have been for the most ignorant auditor in his congregation. As Thomas Hooker expressed it, "The knowledge of the reprobate is like the knowledge which a mathematical geographer hath of the earth and all the places in it, which is but a general notion, and a speculative comprehension of them. But the knowledge of the elect is like the knowledge of a traveller which can speak of experience and feeling, and hath been there and seen and known the particulars." Only one who had been there could hope to guide others on their pilgrim's progress.[1]

Yet the Puritan insisted that this experience of grace must be harnessed to learning if the minister was to succeed in the task to which God had called him. He scorned the view of the "[m]any weak and slight wits in these days [who] think it is as easy to preach as to play, and so they hop from one thing to another and those that are not qualified for the least and lowest employment yet judge themselves fit enough for the greatest & weightiest employment in the world." The antipathy felt by Puritans toward the Quakers and many other untrained enthusiasts was generated by their fear of enthusiasm run wild. Though he criticized the value of learning without grace, William Perkins was quick to assert, "Let no man think I here give the least allowance to Anabaptistical fancies, and revelations; which are nothing but either dreams of their own, or illusions of the Devil; for they condemn both humane learning, and the study of the Scripture, and trust wholly to revelations of the spirit." An individual could not achieve salvation by mere rational means; the intellect had a role to play. And so the Reformers called not only for a regenerate ministry, but for an educated one.[2]

Though it would be difficult to disentangle the directions of cause and effect, the fact is that the Puritan clergy of the seventeenth century were brought up in a period when humanism was flourishing, the universities were growing, and education was more widely available. Biographies and autobiographies that illumine the lives of these men show that they tended to respect learning before they were aware of grace. They came to believe that one of the benefits of grace was the enhancement of other knowledge, and they also believed that reason could help them to categorize and understand the nonrational workings of grace in their souls. In practice they subscribed to the belief that clergy should be university graduates. Within the colleges they wished to see candidates for the ministry trained in grammar, logic, the arts of rhetoric, and the learned ancient languages that would give them deeper access to the Scriptures. In the case of logic they were attracted to the views of the French philosopher Pierre de la Ramée, (known by his Latin name, Petrus Ramus). Ramist approaches were based on the Platonic concept that the natural world is a reflection of the divine mind and that logic is a tool for making the connections clear. His rhetorical theory called for stripping delivery down to a "natural" and simple starkness that discovered rather than invented meanings. Aspirants for the ministry were, of course, directed to mastery of the Scriptures, which study included extensive reading of commentaries and learning the history of both the ancient world in which the scriptural events unfolded and the historical context within which the commentators and other theologians had written. This agenda for learning, first undertaken in the universities, was to be the basis for lifetime learning, and few if any Puritan clergymen were without at least a small room to use for a study. Here again the importance of the new literacy and the expansion of publishing are key elements in understanding the life of the clergy. Supplementing this ongoing self-education were organized exercises for dialogue as a means of continuing education. From the Elizabethan prophesyings to the consociations of the seventeenth century, it was characteristic of the clergy to gather with their peers for mutual edification.[3]

It became commonplace for a Puritan graduate who aspired to the ministry to continue his training in the home of an established clerical figure. John Cotton entertained numerous such young men in Boston, Lincolnshire, and Thomas Hooker's "seminary" in Essex became equally well known. The practice would be carried over to New England, where, for example, young Increase Mather would board with John Norton. In such settings the master would help the novice to mature in godliness as well as in humane learning, working to nurture piety and to develop pastoral skills. Opportunities to travel and listen to other noted preachers also helped to round out the preparation of the minister. One of the key features of lecture days in both Englands was a prominent clergyman delivering a sermon on a day when others were not called upon to preach. This enabled ministers in the area to gather to listen to one of their own.

The challenges facing the newly installed clergyman were many, starting with the difficult question of how to define his task in respect to his own congregation. Though he believed that salvation was limited to the elect and that the list of the regenerate had been predestined from eternity and was beyond alteration, his calling was to preach to all. Joined with a belief in the communion of elect saints was a belief shared by most Puritans of the late Elizabethan and early Stuart era that England itself was an elect nation—not in the sense that all English men and women would be saved, but that the social nation should and could be reformed and that even the reprobate could be improved by instruction. This called for pitching sermons to the broad spectrum of attenders. But the minister was also charged by God with being the means by which grace was transferred to the unregenerate elect and sustained in the regenerate. This task in reality was twofold, for the stimulation of faith called for a different approach—often stressing the terror of the law—than was required for the nurture of the godly. Examination of Puritan preaching and writings will demonstrate how different clergymen responded to these tasks. Indeed, what have often been seen as differences in belief among Puritans are frequently attributable to the audience on which different clergymen chose to focus.[4]

Complicating the task for the clergyman, especially after the ascendancy of William Laud, were a series of practical considerations. Elements of Puritan belief and practice were increasingly defined as heterodox and as grounds for the administration of ecclesiastical discipline or even deprivation. In their efforts to carry on their ministries, Puritan preachers were caught between the expectations of the godly that they would lead, making no compromises, and the likelihood that if they went too far in their dissent from the Laudian church other members of their congregations would report them to the authorities. For those who preached only—serving, for instance, as lecturers—this conflict had been less of a threat since their position did not require them to officiate in questioned ceremonies and practices, but even the relative independence of lecturers was curtailed by the authorities in the 1620s and 1630s.

For those who sought to reach beyond their parochial audience by printing their views, a whole other set of obstacles presented itself. Under Henry VIII, books printed in England had to be reviewed before publication and approved by the monarch, a privy councillor, or one of the bishops. By the end of Elizabeth's reign the system had been further elaborated. The Injunctions of 1559 stipulated that approval of printed material had to be granted by the monarch, six members of the privy council, or any two church leaders, defined as the archbishops of Canterbury and York, the chancellors of the two universities, the bishop of London, and the bishop and archdeacon of the place of printing. In 1557 the Stationer's Company had been chartered and its tasks defined so as to establish another safeguard in printing. No book could be published until it had been licensed by authority as stipulated above. Books that had passed that hurdle had to be "allowed" by two of the wardens of the Stationer's Company and entered in the Stationer's Register. The printer's name was required to be on the volume. The system was constantly being refined to provide greater controls. In 1576 the Stationer's Company appointed 12 pairs of searchers to inspect London print houses weekly to detect illicit printing. In 1596 official licensing was simplified and centralized by placing authority for approval specifically in the hands of the archbishop of Canterbury and the bishop of London (the latter because after 1586 there was no legal printing outside of London). In 1637 the number of authorized printers was reduced to 20 to allow for stricter supervision.

One means of evading censorship was to have works published overseas. The establishment of Puritan exiles in the Netherlands led to the development of a strong publishing presence and resultant efforts to smuggle illicit books into England, though distribution of such works to a large audience was unlikely. William Ames, who taught at the University of Franeker after being driven out of Cambridge, published his major works there. Hugh Peter and John Davenport would be among those to publish in the Netherlands.

While it was possible by such means to circumvent efforts to control ideas, and while occasionally one could find printers in England who would risk violating the law, such actions carried real risks, as Christopher Hill has reminded us, especially under Laud. The Rev. Alexander Leighton was whipped and branded, had his ears cropped and his nose slit, and was imprisoned for life in 1630. William Prynne had his ears cropped on two occasions (1634 and 1637) and suffered imprisonment; Dr. Henry Burton and the Rev. William Bastwick lost their ears in 1637 and were sentenced to life imprisonment. The danger involved in expressing dissent from the pulpit or in print was one of the vital aspects of the culture in which clergy such as Davenport, Cotton, and Hooker learned to survive. The ways they found to express themselves should force us to rethink our concept of "authorship" as it applies to this period. Too often we conceive of authorship as related to the production of published works. But such neat distinctions are not possible.[5]

Those who came to America objected to the criteria being used by English censors of the time, but not to the principle of regulation. It was not until around 1640 that a printing press was established in Massachusetts. Its capacity was limited, but it was nevertheless regulated; in 1662 what seems to have been informal practice was made official with the passage of legislation that charged four ministers with the "power to allow or prohibit printing." During the 1640s and 1650s most of the works produced were for local usage—the Indian Bible and the *Bay Psalm Book,* for instance. The colonial clergy were aiming their publications at an English audience and so preferred publication in London. In the decades after the Restoration publication of colonial works in England became less common—in part, as a result of reimposed censorship in England, but also because of the divergent concerns of the two wings of the movement. And in New England the growing divisions that produced new, if informal, criteria for censorship may explain why one of John Davenport's tracts against the Half-Way Covenant circulated in manuscript but was not printed (Hall, 46–47).

Throughout the seventeenth century the primary method used by clergymen to disseminate their ideas remained the sermon. Sometimes it was designed for print publication, but most often it was not. For Puritans, however, the sermon was always intended to reach beyond the immediate occasion. Believers were urged to take written notes of the preacher's arguments, which were meant to be reviewed and savored afresh by the individual alone and also with his family and friends. Numerous laymen developed this skill and were quite good at it. One scholar who has compared such notes to surviving clerical notes of the same sermons has found that they correspond point for point, though the prefatory remarks to the 1654 edition of John Cotton's *The New Covenant* complained of "the diversity of amanuenses, who did take the notes of his sermons, some writing the same more largely and exactly than others." An interesting point in this regard has been made by the modern editors of Thomas Hooker, who point to the fact that in two transcripts of Hooker's *The Danger of Desertion* (1640), "the conjugal point of view is different." They ask, "Could this coincidence be a clue to the sex of the transcriber?" Certainly we must take care in how much weight we place on such sources as evidence of the views of clergymen. But sermon notes were not taken for the use of historians; they enabled believers to review and discuss sermons among themselves. Lewis Bayley, in *The Practice of Pietie* (1631), counseled heads of household to take time each Sunday evening to "call thy family together [and] examine what they have learned in the Sermon" by reviewing the key points propounded by the preacher. Gatherings of the elect in English parishes were sometimes organized in the form of conventicles within the parish community, and such groups often reviewed sermons from notes. The practice was carried over into New England as a means of reinforcing the lessons of the faith. We know of groups in John Cotton's Boston and John Davenport's New Haven that assembled to review and deliberate on the meanings of sermons.[6]

When it was dangerous for large groups to gather, such as in England under the Clarendon Codes, this practice could be further refined—as when followers of Obadiah Grew, having transcribed one of his sermons, "read to four or more writers in short-hand, every Saturday night or Lord's day morning; and every one of these read it to four men who transcribed it also: and so it was afterwards read at twenty several meetings." While other examples do not reveal quite the same degree of organization, there is ample evidence that copying sermons and sending them on for the edification of others was common from the late Elizabethan era through the seventeenth century. This practice contributed to the related one of friends publishing an individual's "writings"—namely, his sermons—with neither his knowledge nor an opportunity for him to review the manuscript. Thomas Shepard was surprised to find *The Sound Believer* (1645) in print, but his experience was not unusual. Works by John Cotton, James Allen, and Thomas Hooker were also among those known to have been printed from notes by admirers. Many works of seventeenth-century Puritan divines were first printed long after the preacher's death.[7]

Such publishing practices reveal that in seventeenth-century Anglo-American culture it was difficult to draw fine lines between the spoken and the written word. As David Hall has pointed out, "[I]t deserves emphasizing that spoken sermons were like books, and books like sermons, because people in New England perceived speech and writing as continuous and interchangeable" (42). N. H. Keeble, in his introduction to the calendar of the correspondence of the English divine Richard Baxter, has likewise asserted that "movement between the spoken and written word, in and out of manuscript and print, is a reminder that the converse of the period was not yet exclusively literary and that the printed word had not yet assumed the preeminent authority which it afterward came to enjoy. Such exchanges . . . which involve public disputation, private conference, private correspondence, the publication of private letters, and the composition of letters and tracts written specifically for print, are the product of a culture which has not formulated rigid distinctions between verbal, written, and printed discourse" (xxviii).

Another element in this blend was the manuscript specifically prepared for circulation in that form, though the relaxation of censorship after 1640 made it possible for some of these to reach print. Puritan authors who knew that what they wished to say would not pass the censors had to disseminate their views to friends in this form. Such manuscripts are every bit as much "publications" as printed sermons prepared from a layman's notes without the knowledge of the "author." Thomas Hooker and John Davenport both circulated explanations of their Congregationalist views in manuscript to explain to friends the difficulties they had encountered with John Paget in the Amsterdam church. We know of a number of such works by John Cotton when he was in Boston, Lincolnshire. We know of a work, describing a republican utopia, that was written later in the century by the Rev. Charles Morton—the head of the Dissenting Academy at Newington Green outside London, who came to Massachusetts and took a lead in the opposition to the Dominion of New England—and circulated only in manuscript. But it was not only controversial works that remained in manuscript. Samuel Stone's lengthy "Body of Divinity," though never published, was used and transcribed by numerous theological students. Sometimes—perhaps in Stone's case—distance from a press may have prevented easy publication. But others may simply have felt that circulation of their work in manuscript was sufficient for their purposes. Circulation in manuscript served most of the functions of formal publication. In Stuart England it provided opportunities for clergymen who wrestled with the changing Church of England to test ideas, gain the responses of friends, revise their views, and promote the positions they came to hold within the clerical network through which the pulpit was seeking to transform England. Much the same could be said of the colonies.[8]

Of course, print publication was a major form of expression for the Puritan clergy, particularly after 1640, when many manuscripts from earlier decades were rushed into print to accompany the more current thoughts of their authors. Richard Baxter acknowledged the importance of the preached word for "moving the affections, and being diversified according to the state of the congregation which attend it. This way the milk comes warm from the breast. But books have the advantage," he believed, "in many other respects. You may be able to read an able preacher when you have but a mean one to hear." Other advantages he cited were the ability of the reader to choose the topic he would seek counsel on; the survival of books when preachers had been silenced or had passed away; and the availability of books whenever they are needed, as opposed to the more restricted schedule of preaching.[9]

Yet even after the relaxation of censorship, clergymen did not find it easy to use the print media as they wished. Market forces helped to determine what would be printed and what would not. And what appeared in print often was different from what had been submitted. It was commonplace for writers to disavow views that were published under their name, complaining of "both castration and interpolations used by an hand not mine." Thomas Gataker, one of the most respected of seventeenth-century divines, wondered: "[H]ow it fares with . . . others that print at distance, I know not. But with me, who desires to see every Sheet ere it go of[f], & employ my servant constantly to fetch over & recarry for that purpose, it is a very troublesome & tedious employment . . . . [Y]et all my care and toil herein, will not keep free from divers palpable & material Escapes." Acknowledging that "[t]he author is in some respects deemed the unfittest person to correct his own works," Gataker nevertheless was convinced that, "had the workmen regarded what I had espied & amended, the faults would have been fewer than they are." Confronted with the fact that some publications were printed from notes taken by others and without the examination of the clerical author, that other works were never available for authorial proofreading, and that even when such a review was possible authors found it imperfect, it is hard to understand how modern critics can place the interpretive weight they do on the particular choice of words in printed Puritan religious writings.[10]

Though Baxter would cite it as "a precious mercy . . . that every *Booksellers shop,* and every *market* almost, and all the quarters of the Land, do so abound with wholesome and excellent *Books,* declaring the way to everlasting Happiness" (and the same could certainly be said of the colonies), not all Puritan clergymen disseminated their views in print form. While 42 of the 49 ministers examined in this study authored or shared in the authorship of published works, few wrote more than one book. The percentage of their colonial successors who published was much lower, and that of published English Puritans lower still. Yet scholarship was consistently demonstrated in the weekly sermons of the ordinary preachers, as indicated by the clerical and lay notes of those performances. Indeed, there seems to have been little difference in the amount of preparation that was expected of sermons not destined for print as compared with those that were.[11]

Whether the clergyman was preparing a sermon, a catechism, a treatise on faith, or a work on some other topic, he approached the task seriously. John Preston had written that "[e]very sermon which is heard sets us nearer Heaven or Hell," and the same could be said for written works as well. While it is wrong to situate the Puritan clergyman so firmly in his study that we neglect the pastoral work that occupied much if not most of his time, the evidence is clear that communicating God's will was not taken lightly. John Cotton turned his "glass of four hours" over three times when engaged in what his friend and biographer John Norton recorded him referring to as "a scholars day." Few probably equaled this 12-hour model of a day of scholarship, but that is not to say that others took their task less seriously. Most Puritan clergymen owned Greek and Hebrew texts of the Bible as well as the Geneva and King James translations. Their shelves held concordances (such as that compiled by Rehoboth's Samuel Newman) and commentaries to help them decipher the nuances of Scripture. Most owned works of systematic divinity by the church fathers, the continental Reformers, and English Puritans such as Perkins and Ames. Secular works of history and science were available to some, and most had some copies of sermons whose content and form they admired. David Hall has concluded that in New England ministers "owned, on average, something like one hundred books each" (44). Since we know that cost and other difficulties hindered the import of books into the colonies in its early decades, it is not unlikely that the studies of clergymen in England were even better equipped. All of these could be consulted as the preacher prepared his work, though one of the characteristics of what became known as the Puritan plain style was concealing such learning rather than flaunting it.[12]

Because the typical clergyman preached two lengthy sermons weekly, it facilitated his preparation to dwell for a period of weeks or months on a single chapter or set of related verses from Scripture. The resultant sermon series would have the same sort of coherence as a modern course of academic lectures and would also lend itself to dissemination in manuscript or print. Preparation for writing was not merely a matter of academic research, however. True to their effort to unite the spirit with learning, clergymen sought to spiritually prepare themselves for their task. Harry Stout has referred to the Puritan practice of "self-examination as prelude to preaching." Thomas Shepard recorded in his journal how he would engage in "walking in my study musing on the sermon," examining his own spiritual state as a means of establishing an empathy with those to whom he was called to preach. The meditative verses of Edward Taylor are but an extraordinarily beautiful form of what was a common Puritan practice of meditation as a means of preparing the soul for religious activities.[13]

Perhaps the most extensive discussion of preparing oneself for the process of researching and writing sermons and other spiritual works comes in a letter written by Richard Baxter to a young clergyman, Abraham Pinchbecke:

> The chiefest helps that I have found to get both matter & affection for this work are these: 1. to study well the certainty & greatness of the misery of my hearers till my heart be moved with compassion, & can deal with them as men cast over board that are ready to perish; 2. to converse with them privately till I am acquainted with their states, & the objections scruples & misapprehensions of each man . . . ; 3. to study well my own heart, whose wants & sins will furnish me with matter supposing in common cases that other mens hearts are like my own; 4. to ponder seriously of the greatness & weight of those truths that I deliver to them (of Christ & the life to come &c) & apply them first to myself & labor to bring them to my own heart, before I bring them to theirs, for how can I hope that poor ignorant hearers should be affected with that as a matter of weight which their teacher himself is affected with no more than if it were the lightest trifle; 5. when my heart is very dull,I find it very useful

to take in hand some rousing lively writing (such as Mr. [Thomas] Hooker . . . or any that will most affect me) & to read a little till my heart grow warm; & then I am much fitter to study or to preach; 6. but especially I must have recourse to God through Christ by believing earnest prayer which may revive me when other means do fail.[14]

Having prepared themselves through such prayer, meditation, and readings, the Puritan clergy turned to the construction of their message. Though there were variations in structure and style, those differences took place within a general framework that contemporaries and historians have seen as distinctive.

Chapter 3
Structure and Style

The Puritan strategy for communicating ideas is well revealed in William Perkins's *The Arte of Prophesying,* published in 1592. The goals he set for discourse were clarity, simplicity, and the treatment of holy things with proper reverence. While specifically dealing with the structure of sermons, Perkins's concerns are also reflected in the ways in which his followers wrote religious treatises. At the heart of this approach is the Puritan emphasis on the inerrancy of Scripture. The Word of God as revealed in the Testaments was the basis of all religious knowledge and, properly explained, was sufficient for men. The Scripture message was an adequate guide to the moral law for the unregenerated elect and the reprobate and a special nourishment for the saints, whose possession of grace raised their insight to a higher level. This Scripture focus is evident in the content of Puritan religious writings, in the frequent citations of Scripture to underline truths, and in the fact that even when they used their own words Puritan clergymen evoked biblical images and biblical language. By thus wrapping their message in the folds of Scripture, Puritans also conveyed (deliberately or not) that their words were as beyond dispute as those of revelation.

Given this focus, the clerical author was concerned with structuring his writings to properly convey the scriptural base. In sermons, and occasionally in other writings, he did so by starting with the announcement of a scriptural text to be explained. After explaining the meaning of the passage itself, the minister then stated the specific doctrines he would explore. He often examined reasons for the doctrines, stating possible objections and then refuting the objection. Finally, it was appropriate for him to apply the doctrines through a discussion of the uses they could have for the listeners. Though individual clergymen showed some originality in the ways in which they presented God's message, the basic predictability of the sermon structure they utilized was important. On the one hand, it reinforced the emphasis on the message rather than the medium, and at the same time it helped auditors to follow the development of the argument.

Throughout the process the focus was kept on Scripture. Puritans believed in the overall consistency of the books of the Bible, and in developing their message they frequently drew connections to other verses that reinforced their point or put it in a richer context. This pattern of collating various texts was an important element in the development of the argument.

The use of the plain style represented a conscious departure from the fashion that had won the plaudits of most university fellows. Thomas Allen recalled how John Cotton was torn by this choice after he had been converted by Richard Sibbes. Cotton was one of the more eminent Cambridge figures, and it was "the mode of the University at that time . . . to stuff and fill sermons with as much quotation and citing of authors as might possibly be." His peers warned Cotton that changing to what he believed to be "the plain and profitable way, by raising of doctrines, with propounding the reasons and uses of the same," would hide his learning and "would not only be a disparagement unto himself but also unto the college." By choosing to adopt the plain style, Cotton lost many former followers but gained a greater reputation. Later, in writing the preface to Arthur Hildersham's *Lectures Upon the Fourth of John* (1629), he explained his change: "When scholars furnish themselves with store of other writers, besides the Scriptures, and being little conversant in the Scriptures . . . their divinity proves but humanity, and their ministry speaks to the brain, but not to the conscience of the hearer."[1]

Working within the structure of the plain style, different authors developed different emphases. Perkins distinguished five elements in the typical audience for a sermon: unbelievers who were adamant and unteachable; those who were ignorant but open to the Word; those who had some understanding but as yet no grace; those who were humbled but not yet regenerate; and the saints. Those who, like Perkins himself and most of the other New Englanders, focused on the unregenerate elements in their audience tended to draw out the uses of the doctrine more explicitly. Their focus was sharp and their message clear. Alternatively, John Cotton is the preeminent example of a clergyman who focused more on the needs of those already saved, developing a style that was more allusive and designed to spark the gracious imaginations of the elect. Rather than argue for a single meaning of his chosen text, Cotton preferred to introduce additional scriptural texts to offer multiple meanings for the spiritually enlightened consideration of the saints. Yet he too worked within the general structure of the Puritan approach and could be even more rigorous than most in rooting his language in the Scriptures.

The style of the Puritans was labeled "plain," but that does not mean it was artless. The goal of the clergy in their expository writings was to be clear, consistent, and comprehensible to the ordinary audience, not just the educated one. Lawrence Sasek has described the plain style as "a complex theory of style" best described as "a notion of the proper way to achieve the ideal of instructing and motivating the hearers and readers, a notion in which the ideal of clarity and the respect for the beauty and usefulness of literary arts were joined in a . . . taut bond which pulled the writer toward one or the other at various times." It was not calculated to impress the audience with the author's superiority but to build bridges between clergy and laymen, who together formed the community of saints. In this the Puritans expanded on basic Protestant doctrines—Scripture was to be available to all in the vernacular, literacy was to be universal, and the message of the clergy was structured to unify rather than divide. The resultant sense of shared participation in a communion of saints would help shape the religious and also the social lives of the early New Englanders. Puritans hoped that their words would have a powerful impact, and that desire called for simple directness in preference to frivolous ostentation. According to Charles Chauncy, Richard Dod often criticized those clergymen who, "like unskillful Archers . . . do shoot over the heads, much more the hearts of their hearers, and miss their mark, while they soar so high, either by handling deep points, or by using of obscure and dark expressions of phrases."[2] But if ostentation was to be denied, ornamentation was not, Dod's simile itself being a perfect example of the point. The Puritan archer aimed to hit the heart; though his concept of eloquence differed from that of the followers of John Donne, he did seek to be eloquent. Thomas Gataker spoke admiringly about the ability of his friend Richard Stock to use, among other forms, "clear method, sound proofs, choice words, fit phrase, pregnant similitudes, plentiful illustrations, pithy persuasions, [and] sweet insinuations" (Sasek, 49). Nathaniel Rogers went perhaps further than most Puritans in dressing his message; Cotton Mather would recall that he had been known as "a lively, florid preacher . . . a fisher of men, who came with a silken line and a golden hook."[3] But what little remains of his work still places him firmly in the Puritan tradition established by William Perkins, who recognized the minister's need for the "arts, philosophy, and variety of reading" in preparing to compose a work, though cautioning that "he ought in public to conceal all these from the people and not to make the least ostentation" (Sasek, 54).

Thomas Hooker discussed these matters in *The Application of Redemption* (1656, 1657) and elsewhere. For Hooker, "the Language and Words [should be] . . . such as those of the meanest Capacity have some acquaintance with and may be able to conceive." It was the task of the clergyman to "accommodate his Speech to the shallow understanding of the Simplest Hearer, so far as in him lies, always avoiding the frothy tinkling of quaint and far fetched Phrases, which take off, and blunt as it were the edge of the blessed Truth and Word of God." Effects to be avoided by the exponent of the plain style were "pompous gaudiness, and elegancy of Speech, which after an unsuspected manner steals away the mind and affection from the truth." It was the message that was important. Reaching out to understand God's will was a serious matter, and while some, such as Nathaniel Rogers, were inclined to be more florid than others, Giles Firmin spoke for most when he said, "Silken language suits not those who are clothed in Sackcloth." Anything that distracted the believer by drawing attention to the author's wit or the felicity of his expression detracted from the goal. Just as it was wrong to dazzle the audience with fantastic conceits and puns, so it was important to avoid "all obscure and unusual Phrases, dark Sentences and Expressions, [and] strange Languages."[4] Puritans took it for granted that ministers were well educated and that considerable effort had gone into their work. But, as Hooker explained, "it is the chiefest part of Judicious learning, to make a hard point easy and familiar in explication" (*Survey,* sig b [1]).

Use of similes was very characteristic of Puritan writing, which was often filled with images familiar to the audience. Martial similes were appropriate for those who fought in or followed the course of Europe's seventeenth-century wars of religion or, in New England, the Pequot War of 1637. William Hooke referred to "Fasting and Prayer" as "deadly" weapons, "murtherers that will kill point blank from one end of the world to another," and urged the colonists to use these weapons in the fight against anti-Christian enemies so that "thousands will fall, and never know who hurt them." Seafaring images were frequently used by the first generation of colonial clergy in preaching to their fellow immigrants. Hooker was well known for using images and similitudes drawn from the life experience of the ordinary men and women to whom he was reaching out. He compared God's love to a "sail that carries us on a Christian course," and the gradual influence of grace received through the preached word to the December snow that soaks slowly into the earth, its effect to be seen in the blossoms of May. On other occasions he drew upon analogies to friendship, to the processes of farming, and to parent-child relations. A sports enthusiast as a Cambridge student, he described the fluctuations of assurance by observing, "The ball must fall to the ground, before it can rebound back again . . . ; the Lord Jesus Christ must first dart his life into the soul, before the soul can rebound in love and joy to him again."[5] Next to Hooker, Thomas Shepard was perhaps the best known for imagery; by contrast, Peter Bulkeley employed less figurative language. Like Hooker, John Cotton also drew upon agricultural images, such as when he discussed "all the living members of Christ . . . [as] compacted together, and set into one stock, and root" (*Covenant of Grace,* 173). On other occasions he compared the communion of saints to a musical instrument of many pipes, blown into by the Spirit of God, by whose agency one melodious sound is produced. Images of light were among the most commonly used by authors who wished to discuss the process and effects of regeneration. Education, household chores, trades and crafts—such familiar endeavors were grist for the Puritan author's imaginative mill and often issued forth in memorable phrases, such as Shepard's description of mere formal faith as "like a bucket without a bottom, [which] draws up nothing."[6]

One of the most important fonts of images for discussing humankind's relationship to God was the Puritan's understanding of the relationship between men and women. Aspects of this will be discussed in later chapters, but it should be noted here that in comparing the union between God and man to those between husband and wife and between mother and child, the Puritans managed both to speak to the issues of faith and to shape a new consciousness of domestic relationships. The use of such imagery was not unique to the Puritans, but they appear to have gone further than many of their Protestant contemporaries both in dealing with the theme of espousal and in using female imagery to discuss the deity. Similarly, clergymen felt comfortable adopting either a patriarchal or a maternal style of address depending on the type of message they sought to convey.

Among the common means of directing attention to the significance of Scripture was the use of typology, which served both analytical and rhetorical ends. Associated with many Puritan divines, it involved identifying a correspondence between events and persons in the Old Testament (types) and those of the New Testament era (antitypes). This method of drawing a Jewish book and a Christian tradition into consistency was as old as Saint Paul, but the Puritans took it further than many in that they perceived typological elements in the ongoing Christian era: they found it possible, for example, to view the migration of the chosen people of Israel to the promised land as a type for the Puritan hegira to the New England. Typology was designed both to illuminate the meaning of Scripture and to point to its significance. But it also opened disputes: every biblical figure could be viewed as a symbol, and agreement as to the meaning to be assigned it was an act of interpretation over which Puritan biblicists could disagree.

Art was also employed by the clerical authors as they used repetition, polarities, and incremental lists to build to a rhetorical climax. Hooker in particular was noted for sermons that moved the listeners along in a rhythmically balanced journey to a powerfully phrased conclusion. Another rhetorical strategy used by Puritan authors was imaginary soliloquies and colloquies, which in their preached sermons enabled the clergymen to engage in dramatic role-playing; even in published works it was an effective means to draw the audience into the argument being developed. Still another effective narrative tool that appealed to the audience was the personification of virtues and vices. Thus, Hooker in *The Souls Vocation* (1638) and Shepard in *The Parable of the Ten Virgins* (1660) both describe a character labeled Desire on a pilgrimage in search of God's grace. Though none of the New Englanders would achieve the brilliance displayed by Bunyan in *The Pilgrim's Progress* (1678), personification remained a favorite device of the preaching brotherhood. Thomas Shepard's *The Sound Believer* uses the metaphor of pilgrimage extensively. In a number of passages Shepard developed images similar to those later used by Bunyan, as when he wrote: "Away to the mountains, and hasten from the towns and cities of your habitation, where the grace of Christ is published, but universally despised, you blessed called ones of the Lord Jesus."[7]

Attention to the scope for imagination in the Puritans' ways of communicating their message should not obscure the fact that the imaginative enterprise remained firmly rooted in Scripture. The images, symbols, and similitudes used by Hooker, Cotton, Davenport, and their peers were more often than not found in the pages of the two testaments. Though they focused on those aspects of Scripture that resonated most clearly in the lives of seventeenth-century Englishmen, they remained largely within the resources that Scripture provided them. And by focusing on the message of Scripture, using images familiar to readers of the two testaments, and citing biblical verses to buttress their texts, the preachers employed a truth-enhancing strategy that enveloped their own message with the inerrancy of Scripture.

What does not come through to us on the written page is the fervor with which sermons were often delivered. Indeed, one reason some Puritans had reservations about written as opposed to oral presentations was their concern that the former worked primarily on the judgment and could not succeed as well as a preached sermon in stirring the religious affections. Though many of the works of Puritan clergy were never delivered from the pulpit, it is worth devoting some attention to the style of pulpit preaching they employed. Doing so not only reveals some of the characteristic fervor of the Puritan's approach to his faith but serves again to remind us of the dangers of overintellectualizing Puritan religious life.

It has become commonplace to suggest links between George Whitefield's pulpit style and the eighteenth-century London stage. But historians have not been as quick to explore the impact that changing views of the theater in the age of Shakespeare may have had on pulpit presentations. Perhaps the common assumption of Puritan hostility to the theater has contributed to this oversight, but as we become more aware of how changes in the theater mirrored and caused changes in the marketplace and the general culture, we should look for an influence on the pulpit as well. Early in the English Reformation, Reformed preachers such as John Bale composed and acted in religious plays performed in venues that included churches and schools. The style they had developed for the stage was likely carried into the pulpit. Such plays were performed in the Cambridge colleges at the time when John Rogers was a student. Though as time went on it became more common for Reformers to criticize the new theaters and the professional players and playwrights, it is also true that many Puritan preachers of the seventeenth century were known for the drama of their pulpit performances.[8]

Richard Baxter expressed the challenge facing the preacher when he wrote, "It is no small matter to stand up in the face of a congregation, and deliver a message of salvation or damnation, as from the living God in the name of our Redeemer." Yet some became famous for their skill in doing so. The seventeenth-century biographer Samuel Clarke said of William Perkins that when he preached, "he used to pronounce the word *Damn* with such an Emphasis as left a doleful Echo in his auditors ears a good while after," and that he "was able to make his hearers hearts fall down, and their hairs almost to stand upright." Daniel Neal called Thomas Hooker a "Son of Thunder in the Pulpit," and the same image was used by Cotton Mather when he recalled the reputation of John Wilson as "like John, a Son of Thunder, against Seducers" (*Magnalia*, 1: 312). John Collins heard Hooker preach on Romans and not only believed that the minister "certainly knew what a sinner I had been" but also "thought that I was as good as in hell already." Oliver Heywood, writing late in the century, said that John Rogers used "some expressions and gestures which would now seem indecent; yet the gravity of the man, and general reverence people had for him, rendered them not only not offensive, but sometimes very effectual; his taking hold with both hands of the Canopy of the Pulpit, and roaring hideously, to represent the torments of the damned, had an awakening force attending to it." Thomas Goodwin, who traveled from Cambridge to hear Rogers, later told John Howe that the members of the congregation were "deluged with their own tears, and he told me that he himself, when he got up and went to take horse to be gone, he was fain to hang a quarter of an hour upon the neck of his horse weeping, before he had power to mount."[9] John Cotton, whose sermons seem flat and abstract on the printed page, was said by John Wilson to preach "with such authority, demonstration, and life that, me thinks, when he preaches out of any prophet or apostle I hear him not, I hear that very prophet and apostle" (*Magnalia*).

When he recollected the preaching of his friend Thomas Hooker, Henry Whitefield pointed out that such passion was controlled. Hooker was said to have a "choleric disposition, and a mighty vigor and fervor of spirit, which as occasion served, was wondrous useful to him." But he had, according to Whitefield, "ordinarily as much government of his choler, as man has of a mastiff dog in a chain; he could let out his dog, and pull in his dog, as he pleased." The Puritan minister could console the saint with the message of Christ's love, or he could provide the "strong physic" of terror needed for the corrupt heart (*Magnalia*). The style and the message varied with the audience and also with the occasion. Though few clergy could match the beauty of John Cotton's images of filial submission to God's maternal love, equally few could match the vituperation he mustered against the forces of Antichrist in *The Pouring Out of the Seven Vials* (1642). They could use childlike language in the composition of catechisms and then turn to prepare Latin treatises for an international audience of theologians. True artists of the plain style, the New England clergy crafted their task to the work at hand.

Although it is not possible to fully illustrate the variety of Puritan style by discussing only a few examples, examining two sermons can illuminate some of the underlying similarities and nuanced differences in New England didactic literature. Both sermon publications to be examined were grounded in the same chapter of the book of Samuel. The preachers were friends in England and America but are often seen as representing different places on the spectrum of New England Puritanism. John Cotton's *Covenant of Gods Free Grace* was published in London in 1645 from notes taken by one of the members of the Boston, Massachusetts, church. John Davenport's *Sermon Preached at the Election at Boston, May 19, 1669* was probably prepared for the press by Davenport himself.

The text for Cotton's discourse was 2 Sam. 23:5: "Although my house be not so with God, yet he hath made with me an everlasting Covenant, ordered in all things, and sure." Cotton begins by placing the verse in context. It was, he points out, "part of the last Song or Psalm that ever David penned," a fact that made the psalm, he believes, "more sweet, savory and spiritual." Artfully using analogies to persuade his audience of this point, he compares David's last psalm to "the Sun, which shineth most glorious when it is nearest setting," and also to the experience of the Christian saint, who, "the nearer he comes to heaven, the more sweet and spiritual are his meditations." In keeping with the standard structure of the Puritan sermon, Cotton opens the text, dividing it into three principal parts and examining each in turn.

Next Cotton elaborates on the points he has identified and draws lessons from them. The first of these is "[t]hat there is no godly man [who] keeps so good a house, as to walk with God answerable to their calling." If men were capable of perfect obedience, they would "shine as the Sun in the morning, without clouds," but "we are clouded with many corruptions." Cotton pursues this analogy further in an effort to explain that their failings do not deprive the saints of God's favor. "The grass after Sunshine and rain, hath always green and fresh color. . . . I and my house receive many showers and Sunshines, yet are not we in the like manner fruitful and flourishing?" Applying the point to his congregation, he captures their attention by listing some of the ways in which members of Boston's households fail to live up to their callings. Specifically, Cotton indicted his fellow saints for "failing many ways in righteousness towards one another; the husband is wanting to his wife, in not giving her her due of love. . . . Parents and Masters wanting to children and servants." Offering reasons for such failings in the saints—

including "the mixture of flesh and spirit that is in every man"—he raises and answers objections that might occur to his listeners. Next he
applies these reasons to the situation of his congregation, offering a series
of uses whereby his listeners and readers may learn "to judge our selves
and our families."

The second lesson that Cotton extracts from the text is a reminder to
the "godly householder . . . that God hath made an everlasting Covenant
with him, ordered in all things, and sure." Because "God's Covenant is
not disordered, though we are sinful and wicked, yet God loves us freely,
he will pardon us freely, he will heal us thoroughly; so that we shall not
perish, notwithstanding our corruptions"; Cotton thus would "teach
every man and woman, whatever they do else, to labor especially to
shroud and shelter themselves under this Covenant." How to achieve
the safety of the Covenant was a key concern for believers, and at this
point Cotton uses a series of questions and answers to explain how such
security is achieved. "If," according to Cotton, "you can say, you have
known some of your ancestors [were] in this Covenant, and you have not
refused it, but laid claim unto it, when you understood your selves, it is a
certain sign this Covenant reacheth to you." If one was not from a
household of faith, then "seeing as we were not born free, we must therefore take a course whereby we may become free." Here he draws an
analogy between the community of the elect and a guild or corporation.
"To the end a man may be a freeman of a Corporation," he says, "he
must either serve for it as an apprentice" or buy his way in. But in this
case, "purchase it we cannot." So those who seek inclusion must apprentice themselves to God, "give up ourselves to be bound to this service . . .
submit ourselves to him in all things . . . submitting ourselves to be
ruled and squared by him in all things." Cotton expands on the analogy, comparing the fledgling Christian's uncertainties with those of the
apprentice: "[I]n the beginning an apprentice's service is very difficult;
he is exposed to much hardship, he knows not how to please Master or
Mistress. . . . But all this comes for want of experience of a Christian
mans life, [and] if you can be content to break off from your evil ways,
and with all your hearts cleave unto God, doubtless then God hath made
with you an everlasting Covenant, ordered in all things, and sure." That
such success was the result of divine grace is implicit in what Cotton
preaches, but here he is emphasizing man's role.

The third doctrine that Cotton derives from the verse "is the confin-
ing of David's desire and salvation to this Covenant." This means that
"this Covenant is so complete, that a man needs nothing more to salva-

tion, or to satisfy his desires." Cotton enumerated five uses for the doctrine: that men and women should take comfort in nothing less than the Covenant; that if they have the Covenant they may enjoy other blessings; that with the Covenant they need desire nothing more; that they should take comfort from being safe from all dangers; and that those who are in the Covenant should "make use of it to the perfecting of their salvation."

The fourth and final doctrine that Cotton derives from the text is, "howsoever God deals with our families, yet the Covenant of Grace must be to us the satisfying of our desires and delights, and the sum of our salvation." He explains that though God might suffer us to experience earthly discomforts, "we have our eternal happiness in the highest heaven." Contradicting a twentieth-century misconception of the Puritans, Cotton actually cautioned men not to judge earthly fortunes and reverses as indicative of eternal rewards. He urges his audience to "learn to grow in the Covenant of Grace, though we should never grow great, nor rise high in this world," and he warns parents to take more care over the spiritual portion they provide their children than the earthly portion. Cotton follows with the separately headed "Doctrinal Conclusion," perhaps fearing that the main text of the work was too preparationist. Here he emphasizes that "[t]hese gifts we say are wrought, or created by the Holy Ghost, because they are the fruits or effects of the Spirit of God in us, Gal. 5.22, 23 wrought by his Almighty creating power out of nothing." He also emphasizes that "the Spirit of Faith" is not "transient and passing away . . . but they are preserved in us by the Holy Ghost."

John Davenport preached from the same chapter of the second book of Samuel when he gave the Massachusetts Bay colony election sermon in 1669. Newly arrived from New Haven to accept a post in Cotton's Boston church, he chose as his text 2 Sam. 23.3: "The God of Israel said, the Rock of Israel spake to me, He that ruleth over men must be just, ruling in the fear of God." Though he alluded to ways in which the text could be applied to the everyday concerns of individuals, Davenport chose to focus on the political message of the verse, setting forth as his "Doctrinal Conclusion" that "it is the Ordinance of God, in reference to Civil Government in Commonwealths, that some men orderly chosen should rule over other men: and in reference to the qualification of Rulers, that they be just, ruling in the fear of God."

Contrary to what we expect from a Puritan sermon, Davenport told those assembled that he would not "trouble you with the divers readings of the words, according to the Original, being content to handle them as they are translated; and read in all your Bibles. From whence the Doctrine is collected." He then proceeded immediately to expound the doctrine, turning first to prove that "[t]he Power of Civil Rule, by men orderly chosen, is Gods Ordinance." He first asserts that this "is from the Light and Law of Nature, and the Law of Nature is God's Law." Secondly, civil government follows naturally from the organization of men in "Family-Society." It is only as his third reason that Davenport cites Scripture to buttress his doctrine.

Examining the nature of civil government, he explains that "the Power of Government is originally in the People," that rulers are to be chosen on the basis of evidence of godliness, and that such magistrates must "[r]ule in the fear of God." He then turns to the uses of the doctrine. The first use, or "exhortation," is "[t]o the Freemen, who are entrusted by the Community, to chose Magistrates by their suffrages, to follow the counsel of Jethro to Moses [in] Exod. 18.21[:] 'Moreover, provide thou among all the People, men of courage, men fearing God, hating covetousness, etc.'" The second use is to exhort "those, who by consent of the Freemen, are according to Gods Ordinance, to be invested with Magistratical Power and Authority, to . . . judge righteously."

At this point Davenport proceeds to "add a few Caveats," using the occasion to lament some of the recent developments in New England. Specifically, this section of the sermon was an attack on those who would have imposed on all the churches the Half-Way Covenant, to which Davenport was opposed. It was also an attack on the magistrates who had allowed the Half-Way Covenant supporters in Davenport's First Church to secede and organize the Third Church, Boston's Old South. No one in his audience could have missed his message, and the anger of some of the assembled legislators accounts for the fact that the General Court could not agree to finance a printing of the sermon. But having stirred these partisan waters, Davenport returned to safer grounds. The sermon concludes with a unifying appeal to the past, "a brief reminding you of the first beginning of this Colony of the Massachusetts," from Davenport's perspective as one of the original patentees. Early New England was, as Cotton had once said to Davenport, "the New Heaven and New Earth, wherein dwells Righteousness." God's gospel "brought unto you in its right hand, Spiritual Good Things, through Jesus Christ . . . ; and in its left hand, Riches, and Honor, with Protection and Deliverance from Enemies of all sorts." Remembering these blessings, the colonists should "take heed and beware, that the Lord may not have just cause to complain of us . . . lest you lose by God's punishing Justice, what you received from his free Mercy, lest he remove the golden Candlesticks, and the burning and shining Lights in them, as he hath already many eminent Lights." Therefore, he concludes, "see that your fruitfulness is good, answereth the costs & pains that God hath been at with you in his Vineyard."

The sermons differ in a number of ways. Preaching to his own congregation—whose faith he is regularly seeking to nourish—Cotton deals with questions of faith and assurance as recurring concerns of the Christian life. Davenport, speaking on a special occasion to an audience of assembled magistrates, seeks to instruct his listeners on specific issues of concern to the colony in 1669. His message, in other words, is more topical, particularly in its application. Yet even here, the surface differences mask some underlying similarities in the clerical messages. Both preachers seek to place their counsel in the context of general Christian principles as perceived in Puritan New England. It is Davenport's understanding of the principles underlying the nature of government, of good rulers, and of the proper relationship of church and state that forms the basis for his slightly veiled advice on the disputes of his day. Cotton does not present the general nature of faith and assurance as an abstract matter of belief; he seeks to show that this understanding should lead to change in the practical relationships of everyday life between husbands and wives, parents and children, and others. In fact, in this sermon Cotton addresses the question of Christian behavior far more directly and practically than some commentators give him credit for. He and Davenport each move back and forth between theoretical understanding and applied practice.

Structurally, both sermons utilize the logical order of Puritan presentation. Davenport, it is true, skips a detailed exegesis of the text, but he acknowledges his deviation from the norm, explaining that he is "content to handle [the words of the text] as they are translated and read in all your Bibles." Cotton devoted more time to explaining the words and their context in Scripture. Both, however, focus on the doctrines to be culled from the text. Each sets forth reasons for the particular doctrines, considers possible objections, and answers them. Both sermons apply the doctrines set forth with a series of applications of the message to the condition of the audience.

There are clear differences in the methods used by each author to drive home his points. Cotton uses metaphors drawn from the world of nature; such figures are totally absent from Davenport's discourse. Davenport, however, does call upon natural law to support his doctrines in a fashion that anticipates the arguments of later generations. Unlike Cotton in *The Covenant of Gods Free Grace,* Davenport also uses appeals to historical facts. Both, of course, buttress their cases largely with Scripture, making marginal references to texts and citations of scriptural verses in the body of their sermons. An interesting aspect of Davenport's address is his assumption of a high level of scriptural literacy in his audience. Thus, while most clergymen supplied the words of the Scripture when they cited verses in their text, Davenport often provides only the biblical reference, assuming that his audience can mentally supply the words. In the closing passage of the election sermon, for instance, he says: "Copy the counsel that the Spirit gave to the Church at Ephesus, Rev. 2.5. And to the Angel of the Church in Sardis, Rev. 3.2, 3," assuming that his listeners recalled what that counsel was.

There is little in these sermons to hint at the use of dramatic gestures or effects in their delivery, though knowing the context, we can imagine that the atmosphere was highly charged as Davenport implicitly attacked the magistrates who had allowed a secession from his congregation. As printed texts, both sermons, despite some differences, follow the general precepts set forth by Perkins: they are marked by clarity, simplicity, and the treatment of holy things with proper reverence. Indeed, those features were characteristic of most Puritan clerical prose, whether it dealt with matters of piety, polity, or policy.

Chapter 4

Piety

The literary production of the early New England Puritan clergymen dealt with issues of church organization, with questions of social order, and with the individual's responsibilities to humanity. But the subjects to which they returned more frequently than any other, the beliefs that formed the foundation for their other teachings, were centered on the theological issues of the nature of God, human nature, and the relationship between God and the individual. As Thomas Hooker expressed it in *Pattern of Perfection* (1640), the true subject of "religion [is] . . . the knowledge of God, and of our selves." Drawing upon the traditional teachings of Christianity, and in particular on the Reformed heirs of John Calvin, the Puritans articulated their understanding of the order of the universe and "the knowledge of God, and of our selves." In dealing with these issues, Puritan authors wrote from a common vantage point. While the distinguished scholar Perry Miller clearly went too far in his study *The New England Mind: The Seventeenth Century* (1939) in treating Puritan writings as the product of a single mind, the reaction against Miller has been excessive. Examination of their writings will show differences of emphasis among Puritan clergy of the first generation—some preachers stressed particular points more than others because they resonated more with their own religious experience. But those emphases were variations on a common theme. The clergy themselves and their religious opponents in both Englands saw the New England Way as a broad consensus with a shared foundation in the fundamentals of faith.[1]

Puritan pietistical teachings on conversion and the Christian life were developed partially in response to the challenges of anti-Calvinistic preachings in England in the early seventeenth century. Sermons of the 1620s by Cotton, Hooker, and others were crafted to uphold the Calvinistic understanding of faith that Puritans believed to be central to the true traditions of the Church of England. In the 1620s John Cotton preached the sermons later published as *God's Mercy Mixed with His Justice* (1641), *The Way of life for God's Way and Course*, (1624, 1641), and *Christ the Fountain of Life* (1651). In each sermon he espoused the Calvinist predestinarian doctrines that were being undermined by

Laudian initiatives.   Recognizing the mixed congregation of St. Botolph's in Boston, Lincolnshire, he addressed the needs of those who sought preparatory graces while he fed the elect members of his church the spiritual food to sustain their growth in faith. Most of Thomas Hooker's sermons from this period that were later printed—*The Danger of Desertion* (1640), *The Faithful Covenanter* (1644), and *The Stay of the Faithful* (1638)—reflect his concern that Englishmen had become complacent and needed to have their self-confidence shaken by invocations of the threat of God's justice. Yet in *The Poor Doubting Christian* (1629) and elsewhere he sought to reassure struggling believers by emphasizing the doctrine of the perseverance of the saints.

It was in part because they were less and less free to articulate this understanding in England that the first generation of Puritan clergymen made the journey to New England. In Massachusetts, Connecticut, and New Haven these views became the new orthodoxy, and for the most part they were unchallenged. While church polity was questioned by Roger Williams, and the Baptists diverged from the sacramental theology of the New England Way, the central view of faith and salvation was attacked only by Anne Hutchinson in the mid-1630s and by Quaker missionaries in the 1650s.

The starting place for Puritan theology was belief in a trinitarian deity— "all the three persons are coequal, coeternal, subsisting in, not separating from each other, and therefore delighting in each other, glorifying each other"—and acceptance of the fact that this God is unknowable. As William Ames explained in *Medulla Theologica* (1627) [*The Marrow of Theology* (1968)], "God, as he is in himself, cannot be understood by any save himself."[2] In *The First Principles of the Oracle of God* (1648), Thomas Shepard indicated that it is impossible to "sufficiently conceive of the glory of this one most pure essence" (338). A deity whose nature can be encompassed by the natural understanding of finite man cannot, by definition, be supernatural and infinite.

The most that man can aspire to is understanding those attributes of God that he deigns to reveal to man. Man's understanding of God is, according to Ames, "[a]s he has revealed himself to us. . . . [He] is known from the back, so to speak, not from the face. . . . He is seen darkly, not clearly, so far as we and our ways are concerned." In religious discourse, "the things which pertain to God must be explained in a human way . . . and because they are explained in our way for human comprehension, many things are spoken of God according to our own conceiving, rather than according to his real nature" (83). John Norton recognized the difficulty of theological speculation when he wrote that "pious and pure discussions are a legitimate part of the labour of theologians," yet acknowledged that "we have known very pious martyrs who were not very patient disputants." While auditors and readers might in practice confuse the image of God with the reality, theologians should recognize that danger. This refusal to fix the image of God underlay the Puritan rejection of the use of religious paintings, statuary, and other images. It also underlay their ability to use seemingly contradictory depictions of the deity to illustrate God's varied attributes. An author's choice to emphasize one or more divine attributes did not mean that he denied the existence or importance of other attributes. What at first glance may seem to be fundamental differences in belief among the first-generation New Englanders often were no more than differences in emphasis attributable largely to the different ways individual clergymen experienced the presence of God. John Cotton often tasted the sweet love of God; Michael Wigglesworth was visited most often by images of a harsher deity.[3]

Attributes of the deity are to be found in the Creation itself, the work revealing something of the artist. Additional insight into the nature of God has been vouchsafed to some through direct revelation, though Puritans were skeptical about the likelihood of such gifts in their own time. The course of history also reveals the hand of God and his design. But most accessible is the knowledge of the deity available in the pages of Scripture. Thus the search for understanding took Puritans to the study of natural philosophy (what we call science), to history, and to the Bible. Believing in the essential oneness of God, Puritans denied that true understanding of any of these fields could contradict understanding of another.

In their search for God's nature, many Puritans were impressed with the attributes that spoke to divine sovereignty and power. "The omnipotence of God," according to Ames, "is that by which he is able to effect all things which he wills or could will" (92). His power made and sustained the universe and is the cause of all that occurs. "It is his almighty power," wrote Shepard, "whereby he is able to bring to pass all that he doth will, or whatever he can will, or decree" (*First Principles*, 339). While few Puritan treatises directly addressed the subject of God's omnipotence and governance, his sovereignty is implicit in all that Puritans wrote about man, nature, and history. Such attributes were evoked by masculine images of God as father, judge, and ruler.

But balancing this emphasis on power, the Puritans also devoted attention to God's love. Drawing attention to the natural effulgence and benevolence of God was often, though not always, done through discussion of the feminine attributes of the deity. In discussing God's love, Puritan authors drew upon images of maternal nursing, such as in the title of John Cotton's catechetical work *Spiritual Milk for Boston Babes in either England. Drawn out of the Breasts of both Testaments for their souls nourishment* (1646). Thomas Shepard similarly compared the Christian's longing for union with God to the infant's hunger for maternal love and mother's milk. In England in the latter half of the seventeenth century Peter Sterry prayed that Christ "would be a Mother and a nurse" to the members of his congregation. Though common in medieval Christianity on the Continent, Christ's maternal love had been a rare theme in England, aside from the mystical revelations of Julian of Norwich. But the image was used by Puritans in both Englands and fit well with their development of stereotypical female characteristics, such as submissiveness and sacrifice, as essential parts of the Christian character. Puritans strongly opposed the use of images in church or private worship because they were concerned about the danger of confusing human images of the deity with the reality of God. By taking this position, they also freed themselves from the need to reconcile various attributes into any one "picture" of God.[4]

Puritans believed that each individual is a creature of God who through sin has cut himself off from the promise of heaven and the warmth of God's love. They devoted more attention to the human condition than to the essence of God because, in Hooker's words, "it is most available to make us see our misery, and the need of a Savior" (*Perfection*, 4). According to the psychology most Puritans subscribed to, each individual has three faculties: the understanding, the will, and the affections. This understanding explains why most sermons addressed both the rational faculties (understanding and will) and the emotional ones (affections). Adam and Eve were offered by God the Covenant of Works, whereby they would enjoy eternal happiness in return for perfect obedience. In Shepard's *First Principles* Adam's "transgression in eating the forbidden fruit" was identified as an "exceedingly great [sin], this tree being a sacrament of the covenant; also he had a special charge not to eat of it; and in it the whole man did strike against the whole law, even when God had so highly advanced him." This original sin was caused by "the devil abusing the serpent to deceive the woman" and by "man himself, in abusing his own free will, in receiving the temptations which he might have resisted" (342). For breaking the Covenant, Adam and Eve were punished with pain, suffering, and death.

The Fall had consequences for all humanity, "by the imputation of Adam's sin unto us" (*First Principles*, 343). The very nature of men and women was corrupted. Shepard wrote that this was just "[b]ecause we were in him as the members in the head, as children in his loins, as debtors in their surety, as branches in their roots, it being just, that as if he standing, all had stood, by imputation of his righteousness, so he falling, we should all fall, by the imputation of his sin" (344). According to Cotton's *Milk for Babes*, each individual is "conceived in sin and born in iniquity" owing to "Adam's sin imputed to me and a corrupt nature dwelling in me." The operation of the faculties frequently malfunctions. The understanding is shrouded by the darkness of Original Sin so that man places his sense-oriented desires before all else and as a result is led to sin. But Original Sin corrupts the will, or heart, as well as the understanding. Users of Cotton's catechism were taught that their "corrupt nature is empty of grace, bent unto sin, and only unto sin, and that continually."[5]

The Puritan clergyman and layman believed with total conviction that all people are sinners, and, more specifically, that he was a sinner. This knowledge came from observation of the world, from knowledge of history, from reading the Scriptures, and from each individual's examination of his own heart. Much more introspective than later generations of Americans, the Puritans constantly followed the advice to examine and know themselves. In diaries, in autobiographies, and in personal narratives addressed to their fellow believers they expressed that conviction graphically. All were burdened by Original Sin, which Shepard saw as "the contrariety of the whole nature of man to the law of God, whereby it, being averse from all good, is inclined to all evil." Because of Original Sin, man inevitably is guilty of actual sin, which is "the continual jarring of the actions of man from the law of God, by reason of original sin, . . . so man hath no free will to any spiritual good" (*First Principles*, 343). Indeed, humanity is, according to Hooker, "a company of poor, miserable, sinful, and damned Creatures, sinful dust and ashes, dead dogs" (*Application*, 1:200).

The individual's sinful nature makes it impossible to earn salvation. Not possessed of our own society's optimistic view of human nature and its belief in second chances for those who err, the Puritans believed that all men sin and that justice calls for punishment. God had given Moses commandments for his people, not advice. Transgressions deserve punishment. The "wages of sin," according to *Milk for Babes*, were "death and damnation" (99). Shepard concurred, writing that the penalty for sin was "a double death. The first death of the body, together with the beginnings of it in this world, as grief, shame, losses, sickness," and "the second death of the soul, which is the eternal separation and ejection of the soul after death, and soul and body after judgement, from God, into everlasting torments in hell" (*First Principles*, 343). Humans are "damned because of their own guilt," as Hooker expressed it. By insisting on divine sovereignty, Puritans emphasized that God cannot be moved, his will is not altered, by the pleas or actions of mere mortals. Once a sin is committed, nothing the individual is capable of can induce God to change the sentence of damnation. Any clemency must come from God's initiative, not the sinner's. Thus the Puritans followed early Protestant Reformers in denouncing what they saw as Roman Catholic belief in man's ability to earn his way to heaven through works, prayers, charity, or indulgences. As with Catholic views, those of the Arminians "pluck the Crown from Christs Head, the Glory from his Work, the Praise from his Grace, and give it to the will of man."[6]

Just as justice is one attribute of the deity, love is another. Because of his love for his creatures, God extends to some a new covenant, the Covenant of Grace. To those whom he has selected (the elect) God offers grace, which leads the sinner to a faith that in turn becomes the individual's payment for the gift of salvation and the regeneration experienced through the new birth of conversion. Justification by faith is the subject of the only published sermons of Richard Mather, *The Sum of Certain Sermons Upon Genes: 15.6* (1652), and it is an important theme in the salvation writings of all his contemporaries in New England.

Conversion, which we tend to view as the decision of a person to change, for the Puritan was something that God does to the elect individual, who is the passive object in the process while God is the actor. John Calvin had urged his readers to look to Christ for assurance of their salvation, but Theodorus Beza and other followers of the Reformed way had urged self-contemplation and attention to the signs of God's grace in one's soul as a way of determining whether one has been saved. Early English Puritans such as Richard Greenham and William Perkins emphasized these stages of inner change, and much of the literature of early New England was devoted to explaining the operation of the Covenant of Grace in the lives of the elect. In *The Orthodox Evangelist* (1654) John Norton developed the argument that while God's blessed work of converting the individual is the matter of an instant, that moment normally comes at the end of a series of preparatory experiences.

God's choice of those whom he will save is not witnessed and can only be known by its effects. Peter Bulkeley expressed the belief that, "[o]ut of the whole mass of sinful men, the Lord picks out a few base, poor, despised ones, things of no account," and most clergymen agreed that few are saved (*Gospel Covenant*, Cc3r). For those who are, the early steps on the way to self-awareness of sainthood were generally referred to as vocation (indicating God's work in issuing a call) or preparation (focusing on the elect person's cooperation with that call). Puritans were generally agreed that all people can come some distance toward an understanding of their sinfulness without grace, but that such self-knowledge has no merit in the eyes of God. They likewise agreed that only God can change the sinner into a saint. But most clerical authors urged their readers to avail themselves of the ordinances of the church while reminding them that "all outward privileges, as the hearing of the Word, the partaking of the Sacraments, and the like, are not able to make a man a sound Saint of God." The reason for engaging in such activities was that if one has been chosen by God, reading the Scripture and works of faith, listening to sermons, examining one's state, and the like, become part of the salvation stage of vocation wherein God calls the sinner and offers him the graces that enable him to achieve an awareness of his own inadequacy and total dependence on God.[7]

The clergy did differ in the attention they gave to the value of preparatory works during the stage of vocation, though those differences were perhaps not as great as some scholars would lead us to believe. John Cotton is generally seen as making preparation the least important theme in his writings; he generally ignored such efforts or warned that the emphasis placed on them by others could mislead listeners into an exaggerated sense of their own abilities. But this assessment is based largely on examination of his New England sermons, when he was preaching to congregations of the godly. In his English sermons, published as *The Way of life for God's Way and Course*, Cotton talked of the need for individuals to attend to sermons, to pray for a humble spirit, and to seek God's grace. And in *Christ the Fountain of Life*, preached in Lincolnshire in the 1620s, he pointed his listeners to "the preparation we must make for Christ to come unto us." That the published works of Hooker, Shepard, Bulkeley, and others made more of these efforts may

point to the randomness of what got published more than to a real difference in belief, and it certainly reflects no more than a difference in
emphasis.[8]

Through the grace of God the elected saint would come to feel horror
and revulsion for his sinfulness and a longing for the love of God. Cotton
pointed to the role of the ministry in "revealing the grace of the Lord
Jesus in dying to save sinners and yet convincing me of my sin in not
believing in Him and of mine utter insufficiency to come to him, and so I
feel myself utterly lost" (*Milk*, 99). A considerable portion of Hooker's
pastoral preaching and writing was designed to bring individuals to contrition by alternate invocations of the terrors of hell and the mercy of
God. "Hear and fear then, all you stout-hearted, stubborn and rebellious
creatures," warned Hooker, for sins "have been your pastime and delight
in which you have pleased yourself, so far from being troubled for your
evils that it is your only trouble you may not commit them with content,
and without control. . . . Know assuredly that you will burn for them one
day" (*Application*, 11). Thomas Shepard used similarly vivid images in
writing of the soul's view of "the bottomless pit before it, everlasting fire
before it . . . endless woes and everlasting deaths that lie in wait for it"
(*First Principles*, 346). Peter Bulkeley explained that God "uses . . . terrors
of death to bring them to life and peace" (*Gospel Covenant*, ch. 3).
Contrition results when the sinner recognizes his evil nature and sinful
deeds. Beyond this, the elect are next led to a state of humiliation, when
they recognize that they are not only sinners but so addicted to sin that
the cycle of their offenses can only be broken by the power of God.
Hooker, while trying to bring his readers to an understanding of their sinfulness, devoted much of his effort to breaking their wills and humbling
their hearts. As Shepard expressed it, in doing so "the Spirit cuts off the
soul from self-confidence in any good it hath or doth; especially by making it to feel its want and unworthiness of Christ, and hence submits to be
disposed of as God pleases" (*First Principles*, 346).

One of the common images used by the preachers to emphasize both
God's initiative in drawing the soul to salvation and also the love that
motivated his action was that of Christ as a bridegroom wooing the soul.
God calls the sinner to lay aside self-seeking and pretensions to power
and to submit to his authority in loving fashion. Preparatory graces are
a sign of betrothal. All the soul has to do is accept God's love; "there is
nothing required on our side," wrote Thomas Hooker, "but only to
receive him as a husband." Christ will reward such self-effacement with

the constant love and support expected of a husband. Such espousal imagery is found in the English sermons of Richard Sibbes and in the works of Shepard, Hooker, and others in both Englands.[9]

For those blessed by election, contrition and humility are followed by the actual experience of God's love. The sinner is made just through a conversion experience that many Christians have compared to a new birth. This justification is "the gracious sentence of God the Father, whereby for the satisfaction of Christ apprehended by faith, and imputed to the faithful, he absolves them from the guilt and condemnation of all sins, and accepts them as perfectly righteous to eternal life" (*First Principles*, 346). Those justified are reconciled to God, adopted as his children, and sanctified by his grace. Reaching this point along the road to heaven can be sudden—as it was for Saul in his transformation into Paul on the road to Damascus. But it can also be a less dramatic, more gradual process akin to the growth of the mustard seed in the parable told by Christ, or to the image used by Hooker of the December snows slowly soaking into the earth to produce May fruit.

The union with God through conversion was often described by references to the analogy of marriage, and the ecstasy of spiritual union evoked by references to sexual bliss. The justified soul will seek Christ like "a maid that desires a man in wedlock; she does not desire the portion, but the person of the man, if I beg and die with him, says she, if I never see good day with him, yet let me have him, and I care not." United with God in paradise, the saints will enjoy God's embrace in the "Celestial Bride Chamber and Bed of Love." The Christian soul should display the humility and devotion of a wife and her steadfastness. Neglect of the soul's obligations to the godly spouse was viewed as adultery. But just as a bride is owed support, consideration, and love from her husband, so the justified soul can rest in confidence of Christ's continuing love and support. Through humility and dependence, one is actually empowered by receiving the power of grace through the loving actions of God. By depicting Christ as a concerned husband, Puritan clergy such as John Cotton were able to emphasize his concern and caring for man as a counterbalance to the fear evoked by emphasis on the terrors of God's justice. In his American sermons on Canticles Cotton used the rich erotic imagery of the Scripture to achieve this goal and spoke of sermons as kisses from Christ transmitted through the lips of the preacher.[10] Hooker described the union of the soul with Christ as like that of a married couple, who will seek always to "be together, and have one another's company, and they will talk together, and work together, and the time goes on marvelous suddenly, all the while their affections are drawing on" (*Calling*, 257).

Through the power of the Spirit the regenerated soul is enlightened, able to discern more clearly that which is good and more inclined to pursue it. Puritan authors wrote often about the insight that came to the saints through grace. Cotton and others talked of grace giving the saints new ears to hear and new eyes through which to see truths that were beyond the natural understanding of men. The enlightenment brought by the Spirit bestowed an awareness that was beyond the experience of the unregenerate, unattainable by them and inexplicable to them. According to John Davenport, "[T]he spirit of God brings an undeniable light into the soul, which discovers the vanity of those windings, and turnings, whereof men's deceitful hearts are so full." The light of reason "shows little light, not enough to lighten the room," but the light of saving grace "is a greater and stronger light, like the light of the Sun, which is a full and powerful light. This is only from the sanctifying spirit of God. This light shows the evil of sin, and the good of the contrary." It was as difficult to explain to sinners the truths known to the saints as it is to describe a rainbow to one blind from birth. While most clergymen continued to shape their words to mixed audiences of the saints, the nonregenerate elect, and the unregenerate, John Cotton, in many of his sermons, abandoned the reasoned byways along which most men walked in order to evoke images that would trigger the enlightened imaginations of the elect in his congregation, leading them to further understanding of the supernatural.[11]

Charles Cohen has made an important contribution to our understanding of the Puritans by pointing out that this "elation of entering into grace cannot sustain itself forever."[12] Though they believed in the perseverance of the saints, the life of the justified is, as Shepard expressed it, "[a] continual war and combat between the renewed part, assisted by Father, Son, and Holy Ghost, and the unrenewed part, assisted by Satan and this evil world" (*First Principles*, 347). Sanctified by grace, the saints nevertheless will stumble. But while the unregenerate receive "the eternal curse of God for the least sin, and the increase of God's fierce and fearful secret wrath as they increase in sin," for the elect, "the Lord may threaten and correct them, but his loving kindness (in covering their sins in their best duties by Christ, and accepting their meanest service so far as they are quickened by his Spirit) is never taken from them" (348). Confidence that one was being corrected as a saint who stumbled rather than being punished as a sinner who transgressed was difficult for some to sustain, and doubt became a noted feature of Puritan self-examination. John Davenport's *Saints Anchor-Hold* (1661) was an appeal to his contemporaries to deal with the afflictions suffered by their cause as a sign of God's concern rather than as a punishment, and therefore to view their troubles as cause for hope as well as a call for reform. In these circumstances, conversion came to be understood less as a onetime event and more as an ongoing process. Driven by both fear of God's wrath and a longing for his love, saints were brought again and again to the emotional renewal of the experience of God's grace. Both were necessary, for as Cohen expresses it, "[a] superfluity of the Gospel contributes to laxity, while an overdose of the Law leads to despair" (87).

The life of the born-again Christian is a sanctified life; because his faculties have been renewed, he is better able to distinguish right from wrong, to will to do good, and to feel deeper remorse for his failings. One measure, therefore, of whether an individual has truly been saved is gained through an examination of his religious affections and the behavioral fruit of those affections. In response to the question "How do I know I have been saved?" most New England clergy directed their congregations to self-examination of their lives. Much of the attention given to behavior in works of practical divinity and in the diaries of the godly stemmed not from a belief that works are efficacious but from a conviction that the acts of the outward person can be used as a gauge, albeit an imperfect one, to the inner person. A danger in this approach was the possibility that emphasis on preparation and on the behavior of the justified saint might lead people to believe that they in some way are responsible for their possession of the promises of the Covenant of Grace. Some authors, notably Thomas Hooker, combined their discussion of the role they felt the individual has in the process with vivid explications of the individual's total worthlessness. Their sermons rang with depictions of God's power, his wrath and justice, though they necessarily dealt as well with the consolation to be found in his promises to the elect.

Other authors, such as John Cotton, were seemingly aware that even by stressing the worthlessness and sinfulness of individual actions, preachers like Hooker drew attention to works. Cotton preferred to steer clear of that risk in many of his sermons by downplaying completely the role of man in the process of salvation. He customarily used the images of the Scripture to evoke in the saints the feelings that had initially gained them a sense of assurance. While Hooker and others emphasized the course of the soul's betrothal and marriage to the divine bridegroom, Cotton focused on the ecstasy of their union. Or, at times, he (and others who shared his concern) emphasized God's love by drawing attention to the redemptive suffering and death of Christ on the cross that was the foundation of the Covenant of Grace. John Eliot's *Harmony of the Gospels in English* (1678) was a volume of reflections on those sufferings. Other writers also focused on Christ's sacrifice as a means of emphasizing God's love. Cotton, for example, directed the readers of *The Way of Life* to meditate upon Christ's wounds. He believed with Hooker that the humbling of the heart must come before the infusion of saving grace, but since all change originates from God, he rarely bothered to address the saint's involvement in the process.

One of the great ironies of Puritanism is that a people who insisted that human behavior can earn no supernatural reward established a reputation for high standards of moral behavior. Their own explanation, of course, was that the saints led sanctified lives owing to the transforming grace they experienced in their justification. Others have pointed to different factors, such as the reassurance Puritans gained when besieged by doubts if they could find in their lives evidence of sanctification. But what was the Christian life? How should the saints behave in a world filled with temptations?

Perhaps the best brief statement of the Puritan moral ethic is Richard Baxter's assessment: "*Overdoing* is the ordinary way of *Undoing*." Emphasized here is the belief that even things good in themselves can become sinful if done inappropriately or to excess. Drinking alcoholic beverages was acceptable and even normal, but drunkenness was a sin. Clothing appropriate to those in one station of life could be sinful excess for others. Sexual love between husband and wife was a mirror of the ecstatic union between the soul and Christ, but adultery, fornication, homosexuality, bestiality, and the like were perversions of God's gift and sins to be severely punished. Even prayer, the necessary lifting up of the spirit to God, could be done to excess. For the Puritans rejected the ideal of a monastic or otherwise cloistered life of Christian prayer. God gave people gifts to be active in the world and the challenge for the saint was to use those gifts to the utmost in being the best family member, the most productive laborer, the most conscientious citizen, and the most zealous saint—all without allowing concentration on one task to detract from attention to another.[13]

The Hutchinsonian controversy developed when differing emphases in the views of the leading clergymen on works and grace were exaggerated and then attacked by Anne Hutchinson, who claimed to be following the views of John Cotton. Hutchinson and her followers were troubled by the emphasis that colonial clergy placed on the efforts of individuals in preparing themselves for salvation and the use of behavior as a gauge of the inner life. As a disciple of John Cotton, Anne Hutchinson was accustomed to sermons that bypassed these topics. Believing that John Wilson and other clergy implied the efficacy of human effort, she accused them of preaching a covenant of works and sought to steer colonial Puritanism toward a more spirit-oriented emphasis. Contrary to some popular depictions, the Hutchinsonians were not advocates of religious liberty. They sought to make their viewpoint the orthodoxy to be imposed throughout the region. But in seemingly repudiating the utility of moral norms, they left themselves open to the charge of antinomianism. A synod meeting in Cambridge, Massachusetts, in 1637 condemned the errors of the dissidents. Anne Hutchinson and some of her more outspoken followers were brought before the General Court on civil charges, and when she claimed direct inspiration from God, she was speedily found guilty and banished. Even John Cotton abandoned her when her claim to private revelation implied a questioning of the inerrancy of Scripture.

As important as Anne Hutchinson's challenge was in itself, it was equally important as a catalyst in forcing the colonial clergy to define their views. John Cotton came under suspicion because of the errors of his self-proclaimed disciples, and he met with his fellow clergy on a number of occasions in order to clear himself. *Sixteen Questions of Serious and Necessary Consequence, Propounded unto Mr. John Cotton of Boston in New England, Together with his Answers to each Question* was published in 1644 from a circulating manuscript setting forth one such exchange. Another session was described in *A Conference Mr. John Cotton Held at Boston With the Elders of New-England* (1646). A number of the major colonial works dealing with issues of works, grace, and salvation originated in sermons preached during and shortly after the controversy. Thus, Thomas Hooker's *The Saints Dignity and Duty* (1651) came from sermons delivered at the time in response to the theological and political issues raised by the dispute. Peter Bulkeley's *Gospel Covenant* (1646) was a collection of sermons preached in 1638 in reaction to the controversy. Circulated in manuscript in the colonies at this time, these sermon sequences were published in England in the 1640s and 1650s because of the rise of similar heretical views in the aftermath of the Puritan overthrow of the established church there. Samuel Stone's manuscript "Confutation of the Antinomians" was never published. Thomas Shepard's *Wine for Gospel Wantons* (1668) was a sermon preached in 1645. But it included an attack on the antinomian errors that seemed to be arising in England at that time. The sermon was published in 1668 in Massachusetts when concerns about sectarian excesses had once again appeared.[14]

Quakerism was one of those new heresies. It has often been depicted as an extension of mystical Puritanism, the end product of an evolution that moves from Richard Sibbes to John Cotton to Anne Hutchinson and then to George Foxe. Certainly some individuals, most notably Mary Dyer, did move from Hutchinsonian antinomianism to membership in the Society of Friends. But recently this interpretation has been called into question. The Puritanism of Sibbes and Cotton was firmly rooted in the Scriptures, and David Hall has emphasized the importance of the link between preachers and laymen in New England made possible through their literacy and participation in the "culture of the Word." This world of pulpit and print was not at the center of Quaker life. One of the most distinctive aspects of Quakerism was its downgrading of the book in favor of the guidance of the inner light. At some point the move from Puritan to Friend involved a leap across boundaries, a conversion to a new religious system. Some historians have suggested that those who took this step were more likely than others to be accused of witchcraft. Though there is some logic to that argument, more recent studies have cast doubt on the connection, pointing to the fact that in the families in question those who became Quakers did so after, not before, being victimized by suspicions of witchcraft.[15]

The Puritan clergy attacked Quakerism just as intensely as they had opposed antinomianism. John Wilson had been one of the primary targets of Anne Hutchinson and had pronounced her excommunication from the First Church of Boston. The last Thursday lecture of his life, published as *A Seasonable Watch-Word unto Christians against the Dreams and Dreamers of This Generation* (1677), was preached on Jer. 29:8 (" . . . neither harken to your dreams, which you caused to be dreamed") to warn his congregation against Quaker errors. In *The Heart of New England Rent at the Blasphemies of the Present Generation* (1659), John Norton likened the Quakers to madmen who could not be restrained by reason. His sermon was published at the request of the colony's magistrates, and in it Norton justified the punitive measures that were taken against the sect, culminating in the execution of William Robinson and Marmaduke Stevenson in that same year.

All of the clergy, of course, believed in the value of religious exercises for the elect. While some emphasized the use of such acts as means of preparatory grace and others focused on their use as means of nurturing the born-again saint, all urged attendance at sermons, receipt of the sacraments, Scripture reading, prayer, and the various other elements of the practice of personal, domestic, and communal piety upon their listeners. Puritans distinguished between public exercises and private acts of devotion, though there was considerable overlap between them. Public worship centered on the Sabbath and the church. Thomas Shepard's *Theses Sabbaticae* (1649) set forth in great detail the importance of having a special day to recall the Resurrection and look ahead to the Second Coming. "If," he wrote, "a man's heart be lost in the necessary cumbers of the week," on the Sabbath the Lord was "wont to recall it again to him; if any fear that the time of Grace is past, the continuation of the Sabbath . . . confutes him; if a man's soul be wearied with daily griefs and outward troubles, the bosom of Jesus Christ (which is in special wise opened every Lords day) may refresh him." The early portions of the *Theses Sabbaticae* were given to a lengthy interpretation of the Fourth Commandment intended to demonstrate that there is a moral injunction for religious observance of a recurring seventh day. With one eye on the recent antinomian crisis, he then argued at length that the moral law as given in the commandments is indeed binding on the saints as well as on all others. In the second book Shepard states the case for changing the Sabbath from the seventh to the first day of the week, pointing to passages in Acts, Corinthians, and Revelation as indicative of God's institution of Sunday as the Lord's Day. Proceeding further, in the third book Shepard justifies the New England practice of observing the Sabbath beginning on Saturday evening and ending the following evening. This was the same position taken by John Cotton in 1611 in a manuscript discourse on the Sabbath. Shepard's final book discusses proper observance, including rest from all servile labor and worldly sports and pleasures and attendance at religious services. As was the practice of other clergymen, Shepard, as pastor of the Cambridge, Massachusetts, congregation, presided over the long morning and afternoon services that marked Sundays in seventeenth-century New England. In the sermons preached on that day the theme of God's goodness and man's sinfulness, the story of the drama of salvation, was rehearsed and reviewed for all to ponder. Bridging the gap between public and private worship, laymen often took notes on sermons to review them in private or in domestic settings.[16]

Besides sermons, services included public prayer, the singing of psalms, and the administration of the sacraments. New Englanders earned a reputation as a praying people. Though they accepted the sovereignty of God, they believed that God has bound himself to answer the appropriate pleas of his people. Thus, the Rev. Samuel Whiting of Lynn described prayers as "the Soul's Ambassadors, that are sent to Heaven to negotiate great things with God," and urged his readers to commune frequently and sweetly with God through prayer.[17] Thomas Shepard wrote of the power of prayer to "rule yourselves and families" and to "pull down and raise up kingdoms, [and] dispose of the greatest affairs of the church, nay, of the world" (*Believer*, 267). Whiting's colleague in the Lynn pulpit, Thomas Cobbett, wrote the 550-page *Practical Discourse of Prayer. Wherein is handled the Nature, the Duty, the Qualifications of Prayer* (1654). With an amazing thoroughness, Cobbett analyzed the goals, types, and forms of prayer and the attitude in which it should be undertaken. He reiterated the Puritan preference for extemporaneous prayers as opposed to set forms—also found in John Cotton's *Modest and Clear Answer to Mr. Ball's Discourse of Set formes of Prayer* (1642). New Englanders did away with the formularies of the Anglican *Book of Common Prayer*, and though they accepted the use of the Lord's Prayer—because it was a form given them in Scripture rather than devised by man—they preferred to use it more as a model for their own efforts than as a set exercise of devotion. Prayers, particularly petitions, were often combined with fasts as the community of believers besought God for some special end, such as the triumph of the Protestant cause in the Thirty Years War or the advance of reform in England. God's favorable response could be cause for a day of public prayer and thanksgiving.

Psalm singing was yet another element in the public worship of the Puritans. In *Singing of Psalms a Gospel Ordinance* (1647) John Cotton and Thomas Shepard justified including in church services the singing of songs found in Scripture and, on exceptional occasions, a psalm composed by a talented member of the congregation. They rejected the use of any instrumental accompaniment and suggested the practice of having a leader line out the psalm. Dissatisfied with the translations found in the popular Sternhold-Hopkins and Ainsworth psalters, which they believed often sacrificed meaning for literary effect, John Cotton,

Richard Mather, and John Eliot collaborated to prepare the *Bay Psalm Book*, which was published in 1640. Their concern arose from what they felt were loose translations in the alternative versions; their effort was noted by little grace but greater adherence to the exact words of Scripture. Ten years later it was revised by Henry Dunster and Richard Lyon, who both smoothed the translations and added songs drawn from other books of the Bible.[18]

The Puritans believed that there were two sacraments, baptism and the Lord's Supper. A sacrament, according to Shepard, was "a holy ceremony, wherein external sensible things, by the appointment of Christ, are separate from common use; to signify, exhibit, and seal to us that assurance of eternal life by Christ Jesus, according to the covenant of his grace." Their efficacy was limited to the elect, and the Puritans felt that participation in them should be limited to the saints. In the case of baptism, as will be seen, many saw a conflict between the logic of the Puritan theological position—that it was the "washing away of our sin, and so delivering us from death" and "presenting us clear before the Father, and so restoring us again to life"—and the tradition of infant baptism: though children of the elect might be presumed to be themselves elect, the fact was that many who were baptized never fulfilled that expectation. Logic and practice were more in tune in the sacrament of the Lord's Supper, since the Eucharist was interpreted as "the body and blood of Christ crucified, offered and given to nourish and strengthen believers, renewing their faith unto eternal life." The Lord's Supper was "the sacrament of our growth in Christ, being new born, because it is food given to nourish us, having received life," and it was therefore to be administered often—but only to the saints, and only in a public communion service that united believers with each other (*First Principles*, 349–50). Cotton, in *Milk for Babes*, emphasized the symbolic nature of the sacraments, teaching that "in baptism the washing with water is a sign and seal of my washing with the blood and Spirit of Christ, of the pardon and cleansing of my sins, of my rising up out of affliction, and also of my resurrection from the dead at the last day." And "in the Lord's Supper the receiving of the bread broken and the wine poured out is a sign and seal of my receiving the communion of the body of Christ broken for me, and of His blood shed for me, and . . . of the fellowship of his Spirit" (101).

The clergy exhorted their listeners and readers to habitually engage in various private and family devotional exercises. Puritans engaged in meditation and prayer designed to bring them to union with God.

Individuals engaged in self-examination on a regular basis, and families gathered to confess their sins, pray for forgiveness, and thank God for the blessings he had bestowed upon them. Evenings might see family members gather for Scripture reading and psalm singing. Manuals such as John White's *Way to the Tree of Life: Discoursed in Sundry Directions for the Profitable Reading of the Scriptures* (1647) guided colonists in their private examinations of the Bible. Books such as Shepard's *Sincere Convert* (1641) and Hooker's *Poor Doubting Christian* were especially popular as devotional reading. Although their theological views were controversial, the devotional manuals and practices of these Puritans put them in the company of other divines of their age in a tradition developed by Augustine.[19]

Puritan devotional life was part of a process of self-fashioning, which has recently been examined by Margo Todd. Borrowing strategies utilized by Stephen Greenblatt and Clifford Geertz, Todd has demonstrated how Samuel Ward, a contemporary and friend of Cotton and other New Englanders, modeled himself after examples he found in literature and life. *The Confessions of St. Augustine* was a strong influence on the young Ward, as was the Bible. His reading of those and other texts was mediated by the Cambridge community, and especially by Lawrence Chaderton, William Perkins, and other Cambridge Puritans whom he encountered as a student and sought to emulate. He became part of a Puritan community where communion with fellow saints exerted even more influences on him.[20]

Conference was a valued process whereby Puritans came together to reinforce each other's faith. Saints prayed together as equals and engaged in discussion of their faith. Both prayer and discussion were also involved in catechizing, which was another important facet of the religious life of the Puritans. But catechizing was primarily directed toward those who were weak in their religious understanding, especially youth. Though few clergymen were likely to have shared the experience of Giles Firmin, who on returning to England found in his congregation there "one that thought there were ten gods & two commandments," all recognized the need for rigorous catechizing. Twelve New England clergymen published their own catechisms, and others used popular ones such as Cotton's *Milk for Babes*. Some clergymen would distribute copies of a particular catechism to all families in their congregation and regularly meet with them to review the lessons. In the intervals between clerical visitations parents had the responsibility of drilling their children and servants. In such familial sessions the authority of parent, Scripture, and Puritan faith mutually reinforced each other. Written in a style appropriate for children, the catechisms utilized metaphors that introduced youth to the language of religious discourse and helped to fix a communal understanding of the nature of Puritan faith and the forms in which it was expressed. Cotton Mather related how Ezekiel Rogers used to gather as many as a dozen children in his house in Rowley, Massachusetts, and "exercise them, How they walked with God? How they spent their Time? What good Books they read? Whether they prayed without ceasing? And he would therewithal admonish them to take heed of such Temptations and Corruptions, as he thought most endangered them" (*Magnalia* 1:411). Through means such as this and through the family devotions that all were encouraged to participate in, the Puritan faith was reinforced among the saints and passed to a new generation.[21]

Chapter 5

Polity

Puritanism was concerned with the definition and pursuit of the Christian life. In the early decades of the movement it was not identified with a particular form of church government but rather with a concern that government provide proper discipline. It was only the failure of the Anglican church structure to advance reform that led Puritans to consider and experiment with alternative means of church organization, or polity. When the Laudian authorities forced the Puritan clergy into exile, they moved them outside the effective jurisdiction of the episcopal authorities. Circumstance combined with interest to lead the exiles into explorations of alternative polities. In their congregations in the Netherlands and in New England, Puritan clergy such as Thomas Hooker, John Davenport, Philip Nye, Hugh Peter, and Thomas Goodwin developed a congregationally based system of governance that they would offer to their fellow Englishmen as a better way than that of the established church. While these ideas circulated in manuscript among the Puritan brethren in the late 1620s and in the 1630s, they were rushed into print in the 1640s as the onset of civil war in the British Isles offered the possibility of fundamental structural change in the Church of England. But in contrast to many of the works dealing with piety, few of the tracts on polity originated as sermons, and virtually all were prepared and sent forth by the authors themselves.

In addressing matters of church polity, the primary concern of the Elizabethan Reformers had been to establish an effective discipline. Many felt that this could be accomplished through the aegis of zealous bishops such as Edmund Grindal. When the episcopate not only failed to pursue reforms but became a major obstacle to further changes in the church, Puritans began to take matters into their own hands. Until they were prohibited by the queen, prophesyings were a popular means of furthering reform of the clergy; thereafter, combination lectures, in which ministers took turns preaching in a regional center, continued to serve much the same purpose. Ministers who could not impose a thorough discipline over their parishes often separated the godly into a conventicle for extraordinary devotions, forming in essence a church within a church, occasionally formalized by adoption of a covenant.

Such gatherings of the godly into religious fellowships, whether in a parish or in an Oxbridge college, fostered a participatory form of worship and governance that opened some Reformers to the possibilities of congregational governance. Efforts to extend contact between such groups led to experiments in consociation and flowered in the English classis movement of the late sixteenth century. In the eyes of the authorities such efforts were a plot to replace the episcopal government of the church with a presbyterian system. The government cracked down on Thomas Cartwright and the other leaders of the movement in the 1580s and put an end to their efforts. But it should be noted that the Elizabethan Presbyterian movement, with its emphasis on voluntary cooperation between classis members, had as much in common with later Congregationalism as it did with the Presbyterian kirk of Scotland and later English Presbyterianism.

In the decades prior to the establishment of New England most Reformers continued to work within the church to achieve change. As time went on the godly found that retaining their livings required accepting more and more that they thought undesirable, if not actually proscribed by Scripture. Some who found the compromises intolerable separated from the church. Subject to harsh treatment from the authorities, the Separatists began pilgrimages that would lead many of them to the Netherlands and others beyond the Dutch refuge to Plimoth Plantation in New England. Separatists were not, of course, the only Reformers to leave England for the Continent. John Davenport, Hugh Peter, and Thomas Hooker were among the Puritan clergymen who ran afoul of the authorities and sought refuge in the Netherlands before they migrated to America.[1]

Not only did leaving England eliminate the need for compromises, but it forced Puritans to make decisions on how they were to govern themselves. Those whose experience of godly brotherhood had led them to trust the judgment of their fellow saints gravitated toward the participatory forms of Congregationalism. Those who feared the disorderly potential of unchecked godly laymen sought to establish the more authoritarian controls of a presbyterian system. Arguments over congregational as opposed to presbyterian polity were at the heart of the disputes in the English church at Amsterdam in which Thomas Hooker and then John Davenport were pitted against the Presbyterian pastor John Paget.

Hooker put his views in writing and circulated them to friends in England. Davenport's arguments circulated in manuscript as well but were also printed in *A Protestation Made and Published Upon Occasion of a Pamphlet, Intitled a Just Complaint* (1635), in *An Apologetical Reply to . . . an Answer to the Unjust Complaint* (1636), and much later in *The Power of the Congregational Churches Asserted and Vindicated in Answer to a Treatise of Mr. J Paget* (1672). In Amsterdam both Hooker and Davenport had begun to work out the principles of church governance that they would help to implement in New England. Hugh Peter had a similar experience, restructuring the English church of Rotterdam under a new congregational covenant. These and other clergymen had discussed matters of polity in England, participated in the circulation of manuscript treatises, and formed part of the embryo Congregational movement, which also included John Cotton, Thomas Goodwin, Philip Nye, and others who would bring those ideas to the fore in the 1630s in the Netherlands and in New England.

As had been possible in the Netherlands, those who journeyed to America had the opportunity to shed compromise with prescribed nonessentials and to implement what they felt was the best form of church government and worship. In each community discussion led to the consensual choice of a small group of the godly who would be the pillars of the new church. They prepared and swore to a church covenant and thus became the nucleus of a membership that voted on the merits of all who subsequently sought admission. There was some variation in the standards demanded by various congregations, and in *The Real Christian* (1670) Giles Firmin criticized some of his former ministerial colleagues for raising standards too high and not giving enough allowance to God's ability to work in different ways in different souls. But even Firmin believed in the value of a restricted communion. Not only did the members guard access to membership and the sacraments, they also chose the officers of the church and shouldered responsibility for all ecclesiastical policies. But while the individual congregation was self-governing and sovereign, all congregations aspired to unity in traveling God's way and sought to ensure it by regular contact between clerical leaders and occasional assemblies of church representatives where common needs could be discussed and policies recommended. Rogue congregations were not bound by the deliberations of such assemblies, or synods, but could be influenced through a form of ostracism when neighboring churches withdrew the right hand of fellowship.

The New England experiment provoked fears among those left behind. Some English Puritans worried that lay power had run out of control in America and would give rise to all forms of heresy and unbridled enthusiasm. Furthermore, the claims for the purity of colonial practice seemed to imply criticism of those in England who continued to make compromises as the price for comprehension within the established church. And so New Englanders received letters from English friends who were confused and worried by the reports from America.

Some of the earliest New England clerical publications were responses to these fears. Generally both sides of these exchanges circulated in manuscript among the interested members of the Puritan network in England, the colonies, and sometimes the Netherlands. These works were among those manuscripts rushed into print when the coming of the English civil wars broke the censorship of the press and the opportunity to reform the church, even England itself, seemed close at hand.

John Ball and other English clergy had feared that the colonists were moving too far in the direction of Separatism, and they penned a letter to their colonial friends in the mid-1630s. An expanded version of the missive was later published as *A Friendly Trial of the Grounds Tending to Separatism* (1640). One of Ball's concerns was that the colonists had abandoned the *Book of Common Prayer* and all forms of set prayer in their liturgy. John Cotton prepared an answer, which was published as *A Modest and Clear Answer*. Cotton allowed for the use of the Lord's Prayer and the Psalms, since they were derived from Scripture, but rejected the use of all other written prayers. In fact, he felt that the incorporation of any written prayers into a set liturgy was a violation of the second commandment. The colonial clergy also deputed John Davenport to pen a formal response, which was printed in 1643 as *Church Government and Church Covenant Discussed in an Answer to the Elders*. Davenport's response ranged over a larger field than had Cotton's, setting out the details of the colonial church order and answering systematically the English complaints. He defended the colonial liturgy, order of worship, sacramental practice, standards of membership, and other practices. Ball replied with *A Tryall of the New Church Way in New England and Old* (1644), though his response had also been contained in the earlier *Letter of Many Ministers in Old England . . . Together with an Answer . . . and a Reply*, which Simeon Ashe and William Rathband printed in 1643. Thomas Shepard and John Allen ended this particular exchange with *A Defence of the Answer . . . Against the Reply . . . by Mr. John Ball* (1648). Shepard and

Allen retraced much of the same ground that Davenport had covered but did so more emphatically. "We think," they wrote, that "reformation of the Church does not only consist in purging our corrupt worship, and setting up the true; but also in purging the churches from such profaneness and sinfulness as is scandalous to the Gospel." And they claimed that it was New England's mission to pioneer such a reform, the colonists having been "sent into this wilderness to bear witness to [Christ's] truth . . . even to the utmost parts of the earth."[2]

The colonial position on prayer that Cotton had defended was consistent with the Puritan tradition. Though many had used the *Book of Common Prayer*, they did so reluctantly because they feared that set prayers led to unthinking rote repetition that had no spiritual value. They preferred spontaneous prayers, though they made an exception for prayers found in Scripture, as Thomas Hooker explained in *A Brief Exposition of the Lords Prayer* (1645). Their ability to implement these views, however, disturbed those in England whose own compromises were highlighted by the colonial practice.

Richard Bernard was another troubled English Puritan who had questioned colonial practices. Richard Mather responded in *An Apology of the Churches in New England for Church Government* (1643). Mather also wrote in response to criticisms from some of his former clerical friends in Lancashire, authoring *Church Government and Church Covenant Discussed . . . an Answer to Two and Thirty Questions* (1643). William Rathband responded to Mather's views with *A Brief Narration of Some Church Courses Held in Opinion and Practice in the Churches Lately Erected in New England* (1644). Thomas Welde, who had returned to England as a Massachusetts envoy, defended colonial practice in *An Answer to W.R. his narration* (1644). Meanwhile Richard Mather complained that the Englishman had brought "forth such sour fruit in his old age and that he should dishonor his hoary head in the last act of his life . . . at 3000 miles distance and to draw out the supposed divisions of our Churches who never saw as much as the tops of our chimneys or the shadows of our trees." Mather also prepared the magisterial work of over 600 pages, "Plea for the Churches of Christ in New England," but labored so long over it that by the time he finished the Presbyterian threat had diminished. Though his "Plea" was endorsed by Joseph Caryl and circulated in manuscript, it never saw print.[3]

These exchanges demonstrate that the colonists were still part of a larger English religious community. They had not abandoned their mother country and indeed still labored for its reform by offerings of prayer and advice. The treatises that colonial authors penned in the 1630s were not primarily for New England audiences, who had already accepted the practices that were being defended, but for the benefit of English readers who were confused and worried by what they had heard of the New England Way.

As England divided into civil war and the cause of reform was fought out on the battlefield, in Parliament, and in the Westminster Assembly of Divines, New Englanders had to decide how best to aid that cause. Some returned to their native land. Former New Englanders would sit in Parliament and help lead Cromwell's armies. Established colonial clergymen (such as Hugh Peter, William Hooke, and Thomas Welde) and young Harvard graduates (such as John Collins and the Mather brothers) would take up positions in English parishes and colleges. Others decided to assist from afar. When Cotton, Hooker, and Davenport were invited to sit in the Westminster Assembly of Divines and aid in reshaping England's church structure, they declined—but only because they were persuaded that they could be of more use to the Congregational cause in England as experts from afar.

The deliberations of the Westminster Assembly saw a change in the character of colonial writing. Whereas the polity works written prior to 1643 had been designed as answers to specific English concerns, those of the next decade promoted Congregationalism as the proper choice for England to take. The Long Parliament and the representatives in the Assembly were united in their recognition of the need for change, but divided as to which course to take. Many would have welcomed a Reformed episcopate, but the refusal of Calvinist bishops to take part in the Westminster Assembly left that faction without leaders. The military alliance struck between Parliament and the Scots brought representatives of the northern kingdom's kirk to the Assembly as advocates of a Presbyterian settlement. Opposed to that choice were a small number of Congregationalist Dissenting Brethren inside the Assembly and a growing number of sectarian leaders outside its halls. To preserve unity against the common royal enemy, English Presbyterian and Congregational leaders agreed not to preach against each other.[4]

A few New Englanders, such as Nathaniel Ward, Peter Hobart, James Noyse, and Thomas Parker, favored the Presbyterian way. Ward returned to England, where he lent his pen to the defense of Presbyterianism and was critical of Hugh Peter and Independency, the movement for congregational autonomy. Noyse remained in Massachusetts but published *The Temple Measured; or, A Brief Survey of the*

Temple Mystical (1647), which defended broader Presbyterian forms of church membership. Other colonists, Roger Williams and Samuel Gorton among them, identified with the radical sects. But the majority of the colonial clergy supported the English Congregationalism of Thomas Goodwin, Philip Nye, and others who were personal friends of the New England leaders. Though Goodwin and his allies had themselves experimented with congregational practice in Arnhem and other Dutch communities, they relied upon their colonial supporters to provide proof of the success of their polity. In 1643, when English Presbyterian and Congregationalist leaders were observing their polemical nonaggression pact, the debate over polity was carried on with the Scots and the colonists as surrogates for the English factions. Even when the split became open with the publication of the English Congregationalist *Apologetical Narration* (1644), the colonists continued to play an important role in promoting their polity and practice.

John Cotton and Thomas Hooker, as the colonists with the greatest English reputations, played key roles in this campaign. Cotton defined the colonial task as being "to wrestle with God, that they [Englishmen] might not perish for lack of knowledge, nor mistake a false Church for a true." "Great pity were it," he wrote, "that they should want any light which might possibly be afforded them." In 1641 *A Copy of a Letter of Mr. Cotton of Boston* was published, in which Cotton denied that New Englanders had separated from the true church of English saints. In the following year his *Churches Resurrection, The True Constitution of a Particular Visible Church* explained to Englishmen the nature of the colonial churches. Both of these works had circulated in manuscript in the 1630s and were only now reaching print. *The Way of the Churches of Christ in New England*, written by Cotton in 1641 but only published in 1645, was another explanation of New England practice. But *The Keys of the Kingdom of Heaven* (1644) was Cotton's major contribution to the English polity debate. Prefaced by Thomas Goodwin and Philip Nye, who claimed its principles for their own, *The Keys of the Kingdom* was a scriptural defense of the New England Way. Cotton interpreted Matt. 16:19—"And I give unto thee the keys of the kingdom of heaven"—as Christ's gift of ecclesiastical power to Peter and to each of the apostles. Any individual church that was formed possessed the same authority, and there was no superior power above the congregation. Among those influenced by Cotton's treatise was the young clergyman John Owen, who emerged to be one of the foremost leaders of seventeenth-century Congregationalism.[5]

Various earlier writings and sermons of Thomas Hooker were also pub-lished in the early 1640s. His *Exposition of the Principles of Religion* (1645) was designed to influence the Westminster Assembly in its shaping of a confession of faith and catechism. But Hooker's major effort was his con-tribution to the polity debate and came in response to a series of other works. In 1642 the moderate Presbyterian Charles Herle published *Peaceable and Temperate Plea for Pauls Presbyterie* and, in the following year, *The Independency of the Scriptures of the Independency of Churches*, both of which questioned Congregational practices. Richard Mather and William Tompson, who had known Herle in Lancashire and retained cordial rela-tions with him, responded with *A Modest and Brotherly Answer to Mr. Charles Herle* (1644). Samuel Rutherford countered with the critical *Due Right of Presbyteries* (1644). Mather prepared *A Reply to Mr. Rutherford; or, A Defence of the Answer to Reverend Mr. Herles Book* (1647), but the colonial clergy, as they agreed "at a common meeting," also desired Hooker to respond. His *Survey of the Sum of Church Discipline*, published in 1648, became one of the classic statements of colonial polity.

The *Survey* opens with a historical preface in which Hooker traces the decline of Christianity under the ever-encroaching influence of the papa-cy. Reform had begun with men such as England's John Wycliffe, had significantly advanced with Luther, and was brought to the fore in England during the reign of Henry VIII. The body of the volume is devoted to demonstrating how Congregational practices were the true recovery of the apostolic order of the primitive church. Central to the first part of the *Survey*, in which Hooker examines the essence of the church, is the argument that "the power of the Keyes is committed to the Church of confederate Saints as the first and proper subject thereof" (part 1, p. 195). Part 2 sets forth the structure of an individual church and the duties of its officers. Included is the New England preference for two clergymen in a congregation, a pastor "to endeavor by heat of exhortation to quicken, . . . strengthen and encourage the soul in every holy word and work," and a teacher "to inform the judgement, and to help forward the work of illumination, in the mind and understanding" (2:19–21). Next Hooker discusses the nature of membership, setting forth the colonial justification for limiting full communion to the visible saints and the process whereby the candidate is expected to "give some reason of his hope in the face of the Congregation" (3:5). Finally, in part 4, Hooker discusses synods, recognizing the value and even the need for such assemblies—which he had himself participated in—but only as bodies to advise on doctrinal matters. He rejects the Presbyterian argument for granting to synods ecclesiastical power over individual congregations. Throughout the volume Hooker buttresses his arguments with references to Scripture, but he also marshals support from the works of Augustine, Chrysotom, Ambrose, Calvin, Peter Martyr, Bucer, Beza, and over 40 other authors. The English theologians he cites include William Perkins, Thomas Cartwright, and especially William Whitaker and William Ames.

Other New Englanders also prepared treatises to explain their system of church organization and governance. John Davenport's *Profession of faith made at his admission into one of the Churches of God in New England* (1642) provides an example of the form of conversion narrative required for admission to New England churches. When the Scots solicited the prominent Dutch theologian William Appollonius to attack Congregational practices, Thomas Goodwin and his fellow Apologists sought a colonial response. John Norton was chosen for the task, and his *Responsio ad Totam Quaestionum* (1648) was not only an impressive answer but also the first New England work to be written and published in Latin. In a foreword to the work John Cotton claimed that "[a]s for the author's writing in Latin, this was done deliberately, in order that Mr. Appollonius might understand the book without an interpreter and in order that the main points of controversy might be brought to the attention of the churches of the Continent." But the demonstration of Norton's erudition would also ensure that "no one despise this as the inelegant production of exiled and abandoned brethren, far removed by land and sea, voices crying in the wilderness."[6]

From 1646 to 1648 a synod of representatives from the New England churches met in Cambridge, Massachusetts, to prepare a statement of the region's faith and polity. The resulting *Cambridge Platform* was designed in part for an English audience, the call for a New England synod having cited the needs of "Christian countrymen and friends in England, both of the ministry and others." The New Englanders' statement of faith largely endorsed the Calvinism of the Westminster Assembly's *Confession of Faith*. The colonists stressed that "[o]ur Churches here . . . believe and profess the same doctrine of the truth of Gospel which generally is received in all the reformed Churches of Christ in Europe." More particularly, they asserted their "desire not to vary from the doctrine of faith and truth held forth by the churches of our native country," and so, "for this end, having perused the public confession of faith agreed upon by the reverend Assembly of Divines at Westminster, and finding the sum and substance thereof (in matters of doctrine) to express not their own judgements only, but ours also . . . we thought good to present unto them and with them to our churches, and with them to all the churches of Christ abroad, our professed and hearty assent and attestation to the whole Confession of Faith." The platform of church discipline, drafted by Richard Mather, was published in Massachusetts in 1649, with a preface by John Cotton. Heavily annotated with scriptural references, it set forth the congregational polity much as it had been set forth and defended in Cotton's *Keys of the Kingdom* and Hooker's *Survey*. Copies were sent to England, and in 1653 Edward Winslow arranged for it to be printed in London.[7]

During the mid-1640s it appeared as if a Presbyterian ascendancy would emerge in England. Despite their strong doctrinal affinity with the Congregationalists, the leaders of the Presbyterian cause refused to grant accommodation to the Congregationalists. The latter joined with sectarian groups in the coalition of Independent churches united to prevent such an outcome. Both sides in this alliance recognized Independency as a union of expediency only for as long as needed to defeat the Presbyterian threat. This conflict led to a very complex series of polemical exchanges. Presbyterians tried to dissuade moderates from Congregationalism by pointing to the radical views of the sects and arguing that any form of Congregational independence bred heresy and enthusiasm and that only a Presbyterian system could ensure order. They cited the rise of the Hutchinsonians and Gortonists in New England as proof of that contention. But they also attempted to drive a wedge between the English Congregationalists and their sectarian allies by highlighting New England Congregational persecution of individuals such as Roger Williams, Anne Hutchinson, and Samuel Gorton. Politics dictated that the English Congregationalists downplay their doctrinal disagreements with the sects. They seemed willing, however, to allow their colonial allies to demonstrate the ability of Congregationalism to control vile heresies, though they suffered occasional embarrassment when tracts such as John Winthrop's *Short Story of the Rise, reign, and ruin of the Antinomians, Familists & Libertines* (1644) threatened their standing with the sects. New England radicals such as Roger Williams actually served Presbyterian interests. Williams, recognizing the similarities between American and English Congregationalists, attacked the sectarian alliance with Thomas Goodwin and the Apologists in his *Queries of Highest Consideration, Proposed to the five Holland Ministers* (1644). Williams found little difference between Congregationalists and Presbyterians when it came to toleration.

English audiences followed the exchanges conducted by New Englanders for insight into how their own future would be affected by the ascendancy of the various groups. Thomas Welde's publication of Winthrop's *Short Story* was intended to show that the Hutchinsonian errors had originated in England and were not the product of the New England Way. The tract also demonstrated that when errors did challenge the purity of the churches, the Congregational system was capable of defending itself and suppressing heresy through preaching, conference, a synod, and the support of the magistrate. The Rev. John Wheelwright, Anne Hutchinson's brother-in-law who had also been banished from the Bay colony, was in England and published *Mercurius Americanus, Mr. Welds {sic} his Antitype; or, Massachusetts great Apology examined* (1645), which reviewed the controversy again, primarily for the purpose of exonerating Wheelwright from some of the charges leveled against him.

In 1646 another banished colonial radical, Samuel Gorton, published *Simplicities Defense Against Seven-Headed Piety*, which warned of the intolerance of Congregationalism through an examination of Gorton's experiences at the hands of the New England authorities. This was answered by the colonial agent, Edward Winslow, in *Hypocrisy Unmasked by the True Relation of the Proceedings of the Governor and Company of the Massachusetts against Samuel Gorton* (1646). But the most noted exchange involving New Englanders and the issue of toleration was that conducted between John Cotton and Roger Williams. In 1644 Williams arranged for the publication of *Mr. Cotton's Letter Lately Printed, Examined and Answered* and followed that with his *Bloody Tenent of Persecution, for cause of Conscience, in a Conference between Truth and Peace* (1644). Cotton responded with *Master John Cottons Answer to Master Roger Williams* (1647) and *The Bloody Tenent, Washed, and Made White in the Blood of the Lamb* (1647). Williams countered with *The Bloody Tenent Yet More Bloody* (1652).

In these exchanges Roger Williams articulated the views on religious liberty that have made him famous. He argued for a complete separation between church and state. Mere toleration is not sufficient; true civility and true Christianity can only flourish in a society where all faiths are free—Turks, Jews, and pagans as well all varieties of Christians. His case derived not, however, from a concern that churches might exercise an undue influence on civil affairs, but rather from the fear than any commingling would debase religious observances. Cotton's position was more reasonable than is often depicted, though not one that would please modern sensibilities. Accepting a commingling of the spiritual and temporal spheres, Cotton believed that the state must deny toleration to beliefs that threaten the peace (including Catholicism and antinomianism), to views that violate national standards of decency (such as polygamy), and to practices that violate the civil law. He allowed for the toleration of differing beliefs on matters of polity and on matters of nonfundamental religious belief.

In keeping with these views, Cotton hoped for an accommodation of Presbyterians and Congregationalists, pointing out that the few Presbyterian clergy in the colonies were accepted by the Congregationalist majority. And in the 1650s it appeared as if such a rapprochement might succeed in England. The Presbyterian ascendancy had collapsed, and Congregationalists such as Thomas Goodwin and John Owen were among the closest religious advisers to Oliver Cromwell during the Commonwealth and Protectorate. The Cromwellian state church was largely shaped by the Congregationalists so as to incorporate Presbyterians and Baptists of orthodox Calvinist views. From the New England perspective, events in the mother country were moving in the right direction. Cotton tried to facilitate this development with the composition of *Certain Queries Tending to Accommodation and Communion of Presbyterian and Congregational Churches* (1654), written shortly before his death in 1652.

While moderate Presbyterians such as Stephen Marshall did join with the Congregationalists, diehards such as Daniel Cawdrey continued to oppose all forms of Independency. Cawdrey attacked the views of Cotton and Hooker in his 1651 treatise, *The Inconsistency of the Independent Way with the Scriptures and Itself*. Since Hooker had died in 1647, his Hartford colleague Samuel Stone replied with *A Congregational Church is a Catholic Visible Church* (1652). John Owen completed Cotton's unfinished response and published it with his own views in *A Defence of Mr. John Cotton from the Imputation of Self Contradiction Charged him by Mr. Dan: Cawdrey* (1658).

The 1658 *Savoy Declaration* was an English Congregationalist statement of faith and practice that drew heavily on the New England *Cambridge Platform*. The authors claimed that they had set out what they "humbly conceive to be the order which Christ himself hath appointed to be observed; we have endeavored to follow Scripture light and those also that went before us according to that Rule, desirous of nearest uniformity with reforming churches, as with our brethren in New England." But the same year saw the death of Oliver Cromwell and the beginning of the end for the English Puritan ascendancy. The *Savoy*

Declaration would eventually have a greater impact in America—where it was endorsed by Connecticut's *Saybrook Platform* of 1708—than it would in England.[8]

The Restoration of 1660 cast Puritans onto the fringes of the nation's political life and reduced them to the status of persecuted religious minority. With the audience for their advice no longer in a position to implement national change, New England tracts on polity ceased to appear in print in England. English Congregationalists and Presbyterians such as John Owen and Richard Baxter addressed themselves in writing to issues that had little meaning for the colonists, such as the debate over occasional conformity as a means of retaining civil rights.

In the colonies post-Restoration publications on church order were primarily concerned with the increasingly vexing issue of membership. In the enthusiasm of the 1630s it seemed reasonable to conclude that those who were the recipients of God's saving grace would have a clear assurance of their conversion. Doubts that might arise could be quieted by comparing one's sinful course before conversion with the actions of one's sanctified life afterwards. The notion of a new birth was meaningful because life before and the new life after grace truly differed. Based on this understanding, membership in the churches had been limited to those who could testify before the congregation to their election. Children of members were baptized on the assumption that they too would experience such a change. But those who grew up behind the carefully guarded moral hedge of the typical New England town did not acquire a record of sinful misbehavior against which to measure a new life. For those reaching maturity in the 1650s and later, conviction of election was more tenuous; concerned by clerical warnings against the dangers of hypocrisy, fewer and fewer had the confidence to publicly claim their elect status. While piety and churchgoing remained high, membership began to decline. This excluded more and more newborns from baptism and reduced the rolls of those over whom the church could exercise discipline.

Faced with these changes, Richard Mather and others began to argue for a modification of the New England Way. What became known as the Half-Way Covenant provided for the baptism of children who had so much as one grandparent in full membership. On reaching maturity, those who had been baptized but were yet unsure of themselves would retain a partial membership in the church by attesting to belief in the church covenant. Those who advocated this proposal saw it as a humane way to allow for the baptism of the society's youth and a useful means of maintaining church discipline over a large portion of the community. The new policy was debated and eventually approved by a synod in 1662. A number of clergymen who were not able to attend wrote manuscripts on the issue. They tried to influence their peers but eschewed publication at this stage because they wished to avoid involving the public. But the synod's approval of the proposal moved the debate to the churches of New England, where each congregation was to decide for itself whether to adopt the recommendation. Opponents attacked the proposal as an accommodation with backsliding, a dangerous first step in dismantling the foundations of the New England "city on a hill" because a new generation was too lazy to strive for the standards of the founders. At the center of the resulting debates was indeed the question of the inerrancy of the founders. If their work needed repair on one front, and was thus imperfect, then what else might not be called into question?[9]

Cotton, Hooker, Shepard, and most of the other clerical leaders of the founding generation had died before this debate erupted. Thus John Davenport's *Another Essay for Investigation of the Truth* (1663) carried great weight as the view—in opposition to the measure—of one of the few remaining founders. This reception was enhanced by the inclusion of a preface by Increase Mather, who was freshly returned from fighting the Lord's battles in England and was emerging as the dominant clergyman of his generation. An essay by Davenport also appeared in a volume gathered by Charles Chauncy and published in London in 1662, the *Anti-Synodalia Scripta Americana*. Some English Congregationalists, particularly those, such as Nathaniel Mather, who had New England roots, showed moderate interest in the debate, but any hope of eliciting English authority for the opposition position was soon shown to be unrealistic. By the 1660s, rather than enforce any one position, most English Congregationalists had come to tolerate various views and practices regarding the sacrament.

In support of the synod, John Allen published *Animadversions Upon the Antisynodalia Americana* (1664), and Richard Mather wrote *A Defence of the Answer and Arguments of the Synod* (1664); the latter includes an essay by Jonathan Mitchell. Thomas Shepard, Jr., arranged for the publication of his father's *Church Membership of Children and their Right to Baptism* (1663), which was interpreted as support of the new practice. The younger generation of clergymen generally supported the change. Published election sermons by John Higginson (*The Cause of God, and*

His People in New England [1663]), Jonathan Mitchell (*Nehemiah on the Wall in Troublesome Times* [1671]), and Samuel Danforth (*A Brief Recognition of New Englands Errand into the Wilderness* [1671]) all defended the Half-Way Covenant.

Though the General Court had voted to allow publication of works critical of the synod's conclusions, as time went on the preponderance of published works were on the side of change. In 1664 John Davenport prepared a manuscript defending *Another Essay*, but it was never published. Davenport was called to the pulpit of Boston's First Church by a faction that opposed the Half-Way Covenant, precipitating a major row that led to schism and the formation of the Third Church (Old South) by the supporters of the change. In 1669 he preached *A Sermon Preach'd at the Election of the Governor* (1670), using that forum to defend the old way. But the tide was beginning to turn. Increase Mather reconsidered and came to support the half-way practice. Davenport's death in 1670 deprived the opposition of its dominant leader. Political challenges from abroad and the Indian threat within that erupted in 1675 as King Philip's War led many to reconsider and to see a value in more inclusive church membership. But the warnings of Davenport proved correct. In the aftermath of the Half-Way Covenant came further experiments in broadening the church that brought to an end any semblance of regional uniformity in the qualifications for and meaning of membership.

The Half-Way Covenant debate also brought to the fore again the argument over infant baptism. By allowing baptism of infants whose parents were not assured saints, the reformers seemed to be further eroding the notion of the sacrament as a seal of conversion. Not only did the debate over the issue lead some to support and others to oppose the innovation; it also led still others to accept the logic of the Baptist position.

Whereas Quakerism challenged piety (and has therefore been treated in the previous chapter), the Baptist challenge is best understood as a quarrel over polity. The definition of sacraments as seals of grace rather than means of salvation raised the initial question as to the meaning and purpose of infant baptism. Tradition as much as theology led the colonists to adhere to the custom and seek justifications for it. But the restriction of full communion to visible saints made the practice seem more questionable in the eyes of some. In England most Baptists were Particular, or Calvinist, Baptists. They shared the orthodox theology of the Congregationalists and their polity as well. Consequently, friends of New England such as Thomas Goodwin and John Owen learned to accept and cooperate with Particular Baptists such as Henry Jessey while repudiating the smaller number of so-called General Baptists, who espoused Arminian-style views on salvation. They attacked the General Baptists as heretics and tried to identify them with the horrors of Münster, where radical Anabaptists had established a repressive dictatorship in 1534-35. But some English Congregationalists even allowed Particular Baptists membership in Congregational churches, giving them the right to hold their children back from the sacrament. John Bunyan, though a Baptist, had close relations with John Owen and often worshiped in Congregational churches when in London.

Some New Englanders were willing to allow a comparable de facto toleration of Baptists in the colonies as long as the latter did not seek to proselytize. Even when Harvard President Henry Dunster openly espoused his Baptist views in 1653, he was treated with much more understanding and gentleness than sectaries such as Anne Hutchinson and Samuel Gorton had received. When efforts to persuade Dunster to keep his views to himself failed, he was allowed to move out of Massachusetts to the Plimoth jurisdiction. And his successor as Harvard president, Charles Chauncy, was known to also hold suspect views on infant baptism. Indeed, though the penalty of banishment for Baptist views had been enacted by the Massachusetts General Court in 1642, it was never imposed on 20 or 30 known Baptists in the colony during the 1640s and 1650s. Only when a group of Baptists tried to found a church in the 1660s was the law enforced. The Baptists who took this initiative not only forced the hand of the magistrates but were suspect on other grounds. As revealed in the debate arranged between them and orthodox clergymen in 1668, the Boston Baptists were not clearly Calvinist in their theology, and they were not committed to the necessity of an educated ministry.

Sympathy for the Boston Baptists was fanned by a number of factors. Some of the colonial leaders, including Massachusetts Governor John Leverett, had spent time in England during the interregnum and were familiar with the successful cooperation between Congregationalists and Particular Baptists in the mother country. Leading English Congregationalists encouraged the colonists to be tolerant, as much out of conviction as to further their own struggle for toleration. And the debate over the Half-Way Covenant had generated sympathy among the synod's opponents for those who seemed to also be arguing for the purity of the sacraments. Indeed, much of the concern over the growth of the Baptist movement in the late seventeenth century centered on the threat it posed to community unity rather than on differing ecclesiastical beliefs.[10]

Though the uniformity of the New England religious system crumbled in the latter half of the seventeenth century, the vitality of the Congregational Puritan emphasis on communion remained. Even dissenting Baptists imitated the polity of the region, separating from existing churches to form congregations of fellow saints. The combination of congregational polity and loving communion would become deeply rooted in New England; sustained by the social order, it would also invigorate that social order.

Chapter 6
Policy

The distinctions we make between public and private, sacred and secular, were not known in the seventeenth century. John Winthrop's vision of a "city on a hill" was a vision that encompassed what we would distinguish as a social as well as moral order. And so when Puritan clergymen preached and wrote about the future of England and New England, about the structures of state, about the challenges of the marketplace, and about the value of the family, they were expounding on other aspects of what they viewed as the Christian life.

As has often been the case in history, Puritan reformers did not take their inspiration from a vision of an ideal world not yet experienced, but from a past order thought to have been perfect. Their movement toward a new and better future was actually a move backwards to recapture the order of the apostolic church, a perspective that Theodore Bozeman has labeled primitivism. Their striving for purity in Elizabethan and Stuart times resonated with the sense that "purity" involved not only improvement but going back to the first and unblemished ways of worship. The clergy's heavy grounding of sermons in Scripture reinforced the ability of believers to identify with biblical times and measure themselves against biblical norms.[1]

All English Protestants shared the belief that history is guided by a divine plan and that the Reformation initiated by Martin Luther had reversed the long centuries of anti-Christian control. History was moving toward a bright future in which the old Jerusalem would be a model for new Jerusalems. John Foxe's *Book of Martyrs* told that story in such a way that Englishmen were able to view themselves as having a special role to play in this process. Many, indeed, came to view England as an elect nation, specially chosen by God to lead Christendom into the millennial future of apostolic renewal. The defeat of the Spanish Armada—when, according to John Davenport, "the prayers of God's people prevailed to raise the winds, which scattered that *Invincible Armado*"—and the discovery of the Gunpowder Plot were not simply glorious landmarks in national history, they were mileposts in the progress of reform leading to the ultimate overthrow of Antichrist. Similarly, the failure of

James I and Charles I to satisfactorily support the Protestant cause in the
Thirty Years War led to Puritan parliamentary criticisms that went
beyond mere differences over foreign policy. Laudian innovation in the
church was viewed more seriously because it was seen as a departure
from standards of biblical purity, comparable to the falling away of
medieval Christianity from its apostolic roots.[2]

Each person, family, community, and nation was responsible for
recapturing the true order. England, like Israel in Bible times, was in
covenant with the Lord. It would be blessed if the people fulfilled their
responsibilities and punished backsliding. The nation was to be judged
in its entirety, not just by the behavior of the saints. The godly were to
be inspired, and the ungodly coerced, to live lives of outward holiness.
During the early seventeenth century Puritan criticisms of the nation
were phrased in terms of this Deuteronomic framework of national
covenant. Gradually a more eschatological perspective began to emerge,
emphasizing the imminence of the final struggle with Antichrist and the
promised triumph of the saints, all of which gave added intensity to the
Puritan reform drive.

Enlisted in the armies of the Lord, the Puritan clergy viewed themselves as part of the same struggle that was raging on the Continent.
"Shall the members of Christ suffer in other countries, and we profess
ourselves to be living members, and YET NOT SYMPATHIZE WITH
THEM?" asked Richard Sibbes.[3] John Davenport's answer was clear:
"[T]he distress of our brethren abroad should quicken us to the use of all
means, whereby we may be enabled to help them." He drove the lesson
home by relating the needs of Protestants overseas to the concerns of
friends. "If a neighbor's ox, or horse be in a ditch, we will even run to
help it out," he wrote, "much more if his house be on fire." So it should
be, "most of all, if the danger be the loss of their country, of religion,
families, lives and all" (*Royal Edict*, 24–25).

These same concerns underlay clerical calls for reform of their own
country in the 1620s. Preaching on "The Church's Deliverances" on 5
November 1626, the anniversary of the Gunpowder Plot, Thomas
Hooker drew his listeners' attention to the blessings they enjoyed, con-
trasting the "fire of God's fury [that] hath flamed and consumed all the
country around us; Bohemia, and the Palatinate, and Denmark; when
the fire hath thus burnt up all," while "this little cottage, this England,"
had thus far been spared—"we sit under our vines and fig trees, there is
no complaining in our streets, "our wives are not husbandless, our children are not fatherless." In return, Hooker explained, God demanded

that Englishmen "consecrate yourselves, your souls and bodies, to give up all to the Lord. It is he that hath delivered you, let him have obedience from you. It is he that hath maintained you, therefore give up liberally all that he hath bestowed upon you." God had not "redeemed [England] from the devil and from our temporal enemies [so that] we should live in baseness and looseness, and dishonor him." Yet such backsliding was what was happening: "[S]in is grown universal and common and general, so that corruption is, as it were, crept into every corner and coast of the nation, nay it accompanies every sort and condition of men, in every place, in every village and town." Because Englishmen had been privileged above others, the price they would pay for their backsliding was greater than that exacted from others. "What will become of you that have all means of reformation?" asked Hooker. "The Lord's mercies and ministers and judgments have striven with you. What will become of you when such a creature comes to hell? The devil will make bonfires of him; . . . [the] plagues [of others] shall be nothing to theirs that have had all means, and resisted all means, of grace and salvation." And so Hooker turned a celebration of England's special deliverance into a reminder of the nation's special role and its special sin in rejecting reform. England was "breathing out his last and drawing to desolation as near as may be."[4]

The same sense of urgency is found in the writings of Cotton, Peter, Davenport, and others at this time. It strengthened their determination to resist innovation and fueled their decision to seek refuge abroad. But the migration to New England was not a flight. Writing in the 1640s, John Cotton defended himself and his fellow colonists against charges of having selfishly abandoned England to its fate. "It is a serious misrepresentation," he explained, "unworthy of the spirit of Christian truth, to say that our brethren, either those returned from the Netherlands or those exiled in New England, fled from England like mice from a crumbling house, anticipating its ruin, prudently looking to their own safety, and treacherously giving up the defence of the common cause of the Reformation." He justified their decision by referring to Scripture and to England's own history, pointing out that "[b]lame was not attached to Elijah that once for fear of Jezebel he fled into the wilderness (1 Kings 19), nor to those pious witnesses who in the days of Mary betook themselves to foreign parts in Germany or Geneva" (Cotton Foreword, 10).

Puritans believed themselves to be called to witness, to be shining lights and exemplary models. They looked with respect at individuals and communities that achieved this goal. William Perkins was praised by William Ames, who wrote that his Cambridge predecessor had "for many years held forth a burning and shining light, the sparks whereof did fly abroad into all corners of the land." The town of Colchester was spoken of as having been in Elizabeth's reign a "town [that], for the earnest profession of the gospel, became like unto the city upon a hill; and as a candle upon a candlestick gave light to all those who, for the comfort of their consciences, came to confer there, from divers places in the realm." Writing in England in 1611, John Cotton believed that "in our days the Lord enlighteneth the judgment of sundry burning and shining lights especially in our English churches." It was to live such exemplary lives that Thomas Goodwin and Philip Nye left England for the Netherlands, where they created the "new light that did shine forth in the Candlestick of Arnhem." And it was the same goal that impelled the Puritan errand into the American wilderness.[5]

Many New Englanders focused on these images from the Gospel of Matthew. John Winthrop's challenge to his fellow colonists that they were to be a city on a hill was matched in the writings of many of the clerical authors. Peter Bulkeley identified the settlements as a "City upon a hill, which many seek unto . . . a Beacon on the top of a mountain" (*Gospel Covenant*, 15). John Norton assured his readers that "God gives an eminent measure of light, fit to shine forth to a Nation, or to a world of Churches." John Davenport, who told of having himself been inspired to migrate by reports of "the new Heaven and New Earth," wrote of the colonies' "golden Candlesticks, and the burning and shining Lights in them" (Davenport in Stout, 62).[6]

Those who led the great migration and those who participated in it believed that they were doing God's will. As Thomas Shepard and John Allen explained it, they were "sent into this wilderness to bear witness to [Christ's] truth, [and] it is unto us reward sufficient, that we should witness thereunto, even to the utmost parts of the Earth" (*Defence*, 1). Elsewhere the two defined the purpose of the colonial experiment as being to provide "a manifest attestation to the truth, by professions against the corruptions of worship in use, for the necessity of reformation of the Church."[7] Cotton pointed out that God had led him and his clerical brethren to America because "by the free preaching of the word and the actual practice of our church discipline we could offer a much clearer and fuller witness in another land than in the wretched and loathsome prisons of London where there would be no opportunity for books, or pens or friends or conferences" (Cotton Foreword, 11).

A number of colonial preachers believed that the reform of church and state would point toward the millennium. More than any other New Englander, John Cotton was noted for his interpretation of the prophetic books of Scripture. In his American sermons on Ecclesiastes Cotton urged his congregation to pray that "Christ would hasten his last coming as swiftly and quickly . . . to take them up with himself into the highest Heavens."[8] But it was in his sermons on Revelation that he developed his millennial themes most fully. His *Exposition upon the Thirteenth Chapter of Revelation* (1655) contains sermons preached in 1639 and 1640, as events in England were moving toward conflict. In it he identifies the seven-headed beast of Revelation as the Roman Catholic Church and spends considerable space attacking the pope and his church. He contrasts the concentration of authority in the pope's hands with the devolution of authority into the hands of individual congregations in New England, arguing that "[i]t is necessary . . . that all power on earth be limited, church power or other," and that when power is unlimited, one would "look for great blasphemies; look for a licentious abuse of it" (*Revelation*, 72). These themes were pursued in *The Pouring Out of the Seven Vials; or, An Exposition of the Sixteenth Chapter of the Revelation, with an Application of it to our Times*, sermons preached in the early 1640s. He believed that history was moving toward the triumph of God's kingdom and that New Englanders had an important role to play. It was important that "all that profess they came out of England for purity of ordinances . . . be very circumspect, pure, and faithful." If they failed to do so, "either all England will judge your reformation but a delusion and invention of your magistrates or elders, or otherwise look at you as not sincere but counterfeit" (*Seven Vials*, 21). The final work in this sequence was *The Churches Resurrection* (1642), in which Cotton describes the coming millennium as a time of spiritual awakening, though it could not be taken for granted. The saints had to work with God's grace to bring about the triumph of reform.

If such change was to come, the inhabitants of the city on a hill would have to espouse the Puritan faith and bear witness to it in their everyday lives. The churches established in this new Jerusalem were community-based congregations founded on church covenants. But what of the society itself? The Puritan vision of social order was that of an integrated community such as that set out in John Winthrop's "Model of Christian Charity" (not published in his lifetime). "Society in all sorts of human affairs is better than solitariness," according to John Cotton, who believed that God had appointed "mankind to live in societies, first of family, secondly church, thirdly commonwealth" (*Ecclesiastes*, 44–45). Those brought together must recognize their mutual dependence and work together for the common good. Thomas Hooker expressed this idea when he wrote that "every part is subject to the whole, and must be serviceable to the good thereof." "It is the highest law," he continued, "to preserve the good of the whole; at this all must aim, and unto this all must be subordinate" (*Survey*, 188).

Every society comprises various ordered parts. Each individual has specific roles to play in these institutions. Society is ordered; as John Norton expressed it, "Order is a divine disposal of superior and inferior relations, in humane or Christian societies."[9] It was this order that gave strength to the whole, for, as Hooker expressed it, "[i]n the building, if the parts be neither mortised nor braced, as there will be little beauty so there can be no strength" (*Survey*, 188). As in a building, each individual has a place and needs to be connected to others. This appears to be a conservative philosophy, relegating individuals to subordination, denying them advancement. Yet such an effect was tempered in various ways. The sting was taken from subordination by the assertion that those in authority are there owing to no superior merit of their own but merely to serve society's need for different people to perform different and equally necessary functions. As William Hubbard expressed it, "[T]he poor and the rich meet together, the Lord is the maker of them both. The Almighty hath appointed her that sits behind the mill, as well as him that rules on the throne." Furthermore, the emphasis placed by Puritans on the Protestant belief in the individual's direct relationship with God tended to work against notions of subordination. The communion of saints was a society of equals, and the congregational polity was founded on the belief that the elect were competent to decide issues for themselves. The Puritan approach was to allow participation in society but to expect those participating to show deference to the views of their betters. But often they were surprised at the consequences, as when Richard Mather's own Dorchester congregation consistently rejected adoption in their church of Mather's Half-Way Covenant proposal.[10]

The foundation stone upon which all other social institutions rested was the family, often referred to as a "little commonwealth," or a "little church." Applying covenant concepts to the relationship between husband and wife, the Puritans offered fresh perspectives on marriage that placed a new emphasis on mutuality and the duty to love. The earliest expressions of these views are to be found in works such as William Perkins's *Christian Oeconomie* (1609) and William Gouge's massive 1,700-page treatise *Of Domestical Duties* (1622). Marriage, as depicted by these and other clerical authors, was to be both hierarchical and affectionate. Affection was emphasized by Daniel Rogers when he wrote, "Husbands and wives should be as two sweet friends, bred under one constellation, tempered by an influence from heaven, whereof neither can give any great reason, save that mercy and providence first made them so, and then made their match; Saying, see, God hath determined us out of this vast world, each for other." Thomas Hooker believed that a married couple should seek always to "be together, and have one another's company, and they will talk together, and work together, and the time goes on marvelous suddenly, all the while their affections are drawing on" (*Calling*, 257). The relationship was enhanced by the commonplace Puritan analogy drawn between the marriage bond and the soul's union with Christ, as when Hooker wrote that, what the husband is to the wife, the soul is to Christ (*Souls Exaltation*, 77). Thomas Shepard used the example of how "wives mourn for the long absence of their beloved husbands, because they know them, and their worth," to explain the saint's sorrow if Christ seems to withdraw his love. John Cotton used the erotic poetry of Canticles to speak of God's love and of that between husband and wife.[11]

Hooker wrote of a husband's affection for his wife and of how "all he hath, is at her command; all he can do, is wholly improved for her content and comfort; she lies in his bosom, and his heart trusts in her, which forces all to confess, that the stream of his affection, like a mighty current, runs with full tide and strength." Puritan preaching that identified Christ as the soul's spouse drew attention to the concern and love that the husband should have toward his wife. The other side of the image, identifying the wife with the role of the elect believer, contributed to enhancement of the role of the wife by conflating it with that of Everysaint and to enhancement of feminine virtues, which became defined as Christian virtues. In the hierarchy of the family, women were to submit to the authority of their husbands, but the covenant required that husbands respond with affection and protection. This went beyond mere theory, for conjugal obligations were written into the laws of the New England colonies. Just as submission to God brought empowering grace to the saint, wifely submission brought its own empowerment within the family. And the stature of the wife was nowhere clearer than if she was also a mother.[12]

In the "little church" the parents were the elders. Parents were expected to teach their children to read, to catechize them in their faith, to raise them to a calling, and to bring them up in a proper understanding of their place in society. The mother's role included giving birth, nursing and weaning, nurturing, and disciplining. Puritans used female images of God, as when they compared the divine Word to mother's milk, and attention to God's maternal love enhanced the role of New England's mothers. Of course, the Scripture offered many images of paternal love and discipline as well, and these were used to enhance the image of Puritan fathers. The other side of the relationship also drew the attention of clerical preachers and authors. Sermons and catechisms both directed children to obey and revere their parents.

In the well-ordered society of Puritan New England the church was the institution that gave the region its special character. All were required to attend services in the sparely furnished congregational meetinghouses. There the lessons learned in family circles would be developed in sermons that were then reviewed in the home. The clergy used their pulpits to expound on Christian doctrine, to advise on moral issues, and to enhance the authority of the magistrate in the state and of the parents in the family.

The creation of schools was a natural outcome of the clergy's belief in the importance of learning. Dame schools and elementary schools taught Puritan values as well as the ability to read. One of John Eliot's accomplishments was the founding of the Roxbury Latin School. Other clergymen doubled as schoolmasters, and Ezekiel Cheever, trained for the ministry, gained his great fame as a teacher in New Haven, Ipswich, Charlestown, and finally, the Boston Latin School. He prepared his own textbook for Latin instruction, which was often copied and eventually published.

The pinnacle of the educational system was Harvard College, established in 1636. In the section of *New Englands First Fruits* (1643) dealing with the college, Thomas Welde wrote, "After God had carried us safe to New England, and we had builded our houses, provided necessaries for our livelihood, reared convenient places for God's worship, and settled the Civil Government, one of the next things we longed for, and looked after was to advance learning and perpetuate it to posterity." Henry Dunster presided over the early years of Harvard, and Puritan clergymen and laymen in England as well as in the colonies supported the college with gifts of books and money. In 1655 a new president, Charles Chauncy, defended the college against criticisms and cited *Gods Mercy Shewed to His People in Giving Them a Faithful Ministry Schools of Learning* (1655).[13]

The town community was another one of the concentric circles that bound the colonists together. Neighbors were united by a common upbringing, attendance at the same schools, exposure to the same sermons, and adherence to a common vision. All of the institutions of early New England were integrative in their functioning, a fact that explains as much as religious differences the hostility colonists felt toward sectarian threats. Baptists, Quakers, and other such groups led individuals to separate from their old religious allegiance and to form new communities that undermined the unity of traditional life.

John Higginson preached that, because "the best of the saints have flesh as well as spirit, they have something of the Old Man as well as of the New" and need government to restrain their sinful tendencies.[14] Other clergy discussed the nature of government, preaching and writing on principles that not only would become a New England political tradition but would persist from the time of the English Puritan Revolution through the Glorious Revolution of 1688, to the American Revolution of 1775. One of the most interesting elaborations of clerical views was that offered by John Davenport in his 1669 election sermon. Davenport believed that the nature of civil government was found in "the Light and Law of Nature," though he was quick to point out that "the Law of Nature is God's Law." Government originated "originally in the people," deriving from their natural right of self-preservation and the banding together of men in civil societies to "put this power in the hands of civil rulers."[15]

When men created governments, according to Davenport, they did not surrender their rights and liberties to their rulers but only delegated to government leaders as much power—"no more, no less"—as they thought necessary to advance their ends. The people "may set bounds and banks to the exercise of that Power." They bestowed authority on government "conditionally . . . so as, if the condition be violated, they may resume the power of choosing another." Yet, having provided a justification for resistance to authority, Davenport pulled back some and urged obedience to all magistrates. Sobered perhaps by the example of the failed English Puritan Revolution, which he had supported, or made cautious by the recognition that his words would be read in Restoration England, he told his audience, "You must submit to their Authority, and perform all duties to them . . . whether they be good or bad"—at least until they could be replaced in the next annual election (*Election*, 6).

Two decades earlier John Cotton had openly preached on the right— indeed, the duty—of resistance. Working on the same assumptions as Davenport, Cotton had justified the Puritan revolt in England and the execution of King Charles I. He drew heavily on biblical precedents: the execution of Amaziah, who "[c]ometh to fall away from God and to bring great and public calamities upon the state"; the example of Jehu, who "had a call to conspire against the king, his master"; and other similar examples. Cotton concluded, "There is a lawful and loyal conspiracy as well as a disloyal and wicked conspiracy, and therefore it is not an unknown thing that loyal subjects of many a state have conspired against those that have been set over them by the Lord, when once they [the rulers] depart from God and do such acts as have been dangerous and destructive to the Commonwealth." In a departure from his usual practice, he added a precedent from history, citing "a wise speech of Trajan, when he committed the sword to any: use it for me, saith he, while I rule according to law and justice, but against me when otherwise."[16]

Both Cotton and Davenport emphasized the importance of just leaders who ruled in the fear of God. From the founding of New England to the Restoration of 1660, the leaders of New England were able, with minor exceptions, to impose their model on those who came to live there. That task was carried out by the colony magistrates. New England was not a theocracy in the sense of being a state controlled by a religious caste or priesthood. John Cotton, Thomas Cobbett, Thomas Hooker, and others who addressed the subject of magisterial powers all espoused beliefs that in the parlance of their times would properly be identified as Erastianism: vesting in the state the responsibility for nurturing the church. But those who held and wielded the civil power were laymen whose views were shaped by the preachings from the pulpit.

Davenport believed that any system of government could serve the needs of a people. An unpublished treatise thought to have been written by John Norton classified the colonial system as a mixture of aristocracy ("where majesty or supreme civil power is committed by the people to the nobles or superior sort of people") and democracy (in which power is committed to "any sort of the people"). Freemanship—the right to vote—was limited in Massachusetts to church members, and they were expected to exercise that right to choose godly magistrates. Thomas

Shepard took the occasion of an election sermon he preached in 1638 to remind the colonists: "[L]et any come over among us never so nobly descended . . . it may be there hearts may be so corrupt and apt to be carried by private respects . . . that [they are] troublers not keepers of vineyards." He warned that no one, therefore, should be chosen for office until "known for wisdom, holiness, [and] public spirit."[17]

One task of the magistrates was to enact and enforce laws that advanced the interests of God and his people. In 1636 three ministers—John Cotton, Hugh Peter, and Thomas Shepard—were named to a committee with four of the magistrates to frame a body of law. Cotton drafted what was in essence an abstract of laws already established in the Bay colony, along with scriptural justifications for them. This was eventually published as *An Abstract; or, The Laws of New England as they are now established* (1641). It went beyond a legal code and provided a blueprint for government that was also adopted by the New Haven colony in 1639. Though Cotton expressed his belief that "tis a part of the happiness of Christian nations that they are subject to the laws of that commonwealth of Israel," the compilation shows as much familiarity with and application of English common law as the provisions of the Bible. Such knowledge generally informed the political writings of most Puritan authors, though John Eliot's *Christian Commonwealth* (1659) proposed a literal borrowing of the political organization of the tribes of Israel. Cotton's chapter explicating crimes and their punishment lists 19 capital offenses punishable by death. This number is actually less than the number of capital crimes provided by common law; in England, as opposed to Massachusetts, one could suffer death for housebreaking, stealing more than a shilling, and a number of other crimes. But some of the offenses that Cotton did include on his list—Sabbath breaking, adultery, and rebellion against one's parents—were not capital offenses in the mother country.[18]

Cotton's code called for the establishment of town committees to regulate wages and prices. This practice was in keeping with the Puritan effort to avoid exploitation of others in the fluid economic situation of the Bay colony. The colonial clergy agreed with William Perkins that an economic calling was "ordained and imposed on man by God for the common good." God consequently expected diligence, so that one should, in Cotton's words, "rise early, and go to bed late, and eat the bread of carefulness [and] . . . avoid idleness" (*Fountain*, 114–15). But, as with any other behavior, too much attention to work and profit distracts the individual from his other duties and responsibil-

ities and leads to sin. Thus the clergy balanced their calls for zeal with
cautions against excess. The church sought to influence proper behavior in the economic sphere, censuring those, such as the Boston merchant Robert Keayne, who transgressed. And the law provided a
further hedge against individual greed that could undermine the common wealth.[19]

The Puritan saint took quite literally the teaching that his neighbor
was his brother and that he was his brother's keeper. There is little doubt
that most modern Americans would find Puritan public scrutiny of what
we consider private behavior intrusive and oppressive. A question that
needs further study is how divisive the posture of the saints was. Some
recent scholarship in England has emphasized that Puritan zeal divided
communities and created social rifts that perhaps influenced allegiance at
the time of the English civil wars. Patrick Collinson has raised questions
about "The Cohabitation of the Faithful with the Unfaithful" (1991) in
Stuart England, suggesting that Puritan efforts to "preserve a distance
between the godly and the ungodly on a day-to-day basis" meant that
"the opportunity for 'familiar company keeping,' ordinary social converse, was, in principle, severely restricted." Collinson points to the language of binary opposition that was common to the religious discourse
of the time and suggests that, by encouraging Puritans to divide society
between "godly" and "ungodly," it contributed to social divisiveness.
There is no question that the efforts of godly magistrates to reform an
unwilling populace sometimes gave rise to hostility against the Puritans,
whether the effort was in John White's Dorchester, as studied by David
Underdown, or the work of Cromwell's Major-Generals in the 1650s.
Yet Collinson himself recognizes this as a subject that needs further
study and has elsewhere pointed to the unitive goals of Puritanism. In
New England such polarities did not seem to exist. The community valued by the colonists was not simply the communicants of the church.
Puritan preachers believed that ultimately all men can be categorized as
godly or ungodly, but when they mounted their pulpits, they viewed the
populace in the pews as falling into a larger number of categories. Some
of those who appeared ungodly might yet by God's grace be brought
into the fellowship of saints. This perception encouraged the clergy to
reach out to the weak in spirit rather than to shun them. Yet whether
this effort tells us something important about Puritanism in general or
merely about those who came to New England is a question we are not
yet ready to answer.[20]

One of the challenges faced by New England Puritans and not by their English brethren was that posed by the Native Americans. Despite the obstacles presented by differences in language and differences in conceptual experience, some Puritan clergymen sought to bring Indians to the Lord. Roger Williams showed understanding and appreciation of Narragansett language and customs in his *Key into the Language of America* (1643). The Rev. Thomas Mayhew labored among the Indians on Martha's Vineyard. His account formed part of Henry Whitfield's *The Light Appearing More and More Towards the Perfect Day; or, A Farther Discovery of the Present State of the Indians in New England* (1651). John Wilson's direct efforts in preaching the Gospel to the Indians cannot be established. But a Watertown Sagamore who converted to Christianity left his son in Wilson's care when he died, and Wilson, who was a friend of John Eliot, wrote the first account seeking English support for the Massachusetts mission, *The Day-Breaking, if not the Sun-Rising of the Gospel with the Indians in New England* (1647).

John Eliot, whose millenialist expectations were perhaps more intense than those of any other New England clergyman of his time, was persuaded that the Indians were heirs of the lost tribes of Israel and that their conversion would be one of the landmarks of the progress toward the millennium. Over and above his ministry to the Roxbury church, he took upon himself the task of ministering to the Algonquian tribes of eastern Massachusetts. Having acquired some sufficiency in the native language, he began in 1646 to journey to Indian villages to deliver sermons and begin a process of catechizing. His efforts were reported by Wilson and then by Thomas Shepard in *The Clear Sunshine of the Gospel Breaking on the Indians* (1648). These accounts and pleas led to Parliament chartering the Society for Propagation of the Gospel in New England in 1649. That corporation raised money in England that was distributed to Eliot, Mayhew, and others.

Structurally, the mission to the Indians took shape in "praying towns" of converts who sought to adopt English cultural forms as well as the Puritan faith, and in the Indian College at Harvard, which was designed to train native clergy. The effort was reflected in print in published accounts of the progress of the Gospel and also in Eliot's publication of books in the Algonquian language. These included *The Indian Grammar begun* (1666), *The Indian Primer* (1669), and *The Logic Primer for the use of Indians* (1672) which were designed to advance native literacy, and his translations of *A Few Psalms in Meter* (1658), *The New Testament in the*

Indian Tongue (1661), *The Assembly's Shorter Catechism* (1663), and *The Holy Bible* (1663).

The social ethic developed by the clerical preachers and authors was designed to give a new shape to the English nation and to the new England in America. The efforts of John Eliot and others were intended to take that model across cultural boundaries. But the hope of such a new day would fade as the 1650s came to a close. There would be no Puritan England, and the days of Puritan New England would be numbered. The Indian uprising called King Philip's War destroyed most colonial outreach to the region's tribes. Yet the values of community and balance that lay at the root of this ethic were values that could be preserved on a smaller scale, and the heritage of Puritanism would continue in the small towns of New England and in the local societies of Dissenters in the mother country.

Chapter 7

Passages

The Restoration changed everything. In England Puritanism was driven from the church and the various groups of Dissenters had to adjust to sectarian survival under the penal Clarendon Codes. New England's Puritans found the autonomy they had taken for granted challenged. New Haven's very existence was ended by a new royal charter granted to Connecticut. The practices of the Bay colony came under scrutiny from royal commissioners. The persecution of Quakers was halted by royal edict. And the dream of a new world order to be initiated by the Puritan example became a hope deferred. If the founders saw themselves as a saving remnant, the colonists of the 1660s and later saw themselves as an embattled remnant threatened by forces without and forces within. From evangelicals hoping to save the world, they turned inward, erecting hedges behind which they could try to preserve the heritage of their fathers and save themselves.

Many of those who had shaped New England were no longer alive to see the Restoration. John Cotton, Thomas Shepard, Thomas Hooker, Peter Bulkeley, Francis Higginson, Nathaniel Rogers, Henry Dunster, and Nathaniel Ward were among those who had passed away prior to 1660. Others had returned to England and remained there, including Hugh Peter (executed as a regicide in 1660), Samuel Eaton, William Hooke, and Giles Firmin. John Norton and Samuel Stone died within three years of the Stuart return. Survivors such as John Davenport, Charles Chauncy, Richard Mather, and John Eliot had to deal with the collapse of the hopes that had sustained them in their English suffering, their migration, and their labors in the American wilderness. Deprived of their expectations for the imminence of a reformed Christendom, they could take solace only from their experience of God's gracious presence within their souls.

From time to time the surviving founders felt frustration at the collapse of their dreams. As Christopher Hill has pointed out, "Men had believed that their Cause was invincible because it was God's. The defeat therefore called into question either God's goodness or his omnipotence, or their understanding of God's will." Indeed, it is no surprise that Milton would feel called upon to have to justify the ways of God to man. The defeated leaders of England's revolution were more prone to such thoughts than the colonists, for whom the changes of the 1660s were not as dramatic. But like an English friend of Oliver Cromwell, they were tempted to feel that in the reversal of Puritan fortunes God had spit in their faces. Increasingly, they looked for sins that might have caused these judgments and joined in preaching the jeremiads that became commonplace in the last decades of the century. In *Gods Call to His People to Turn Unto Him* (1669) John Davenport reviewed the abuses of the times, including a growing observance of Christmas. But most often these preachers showed more interest in comforting than castigating their flocks. They sought to sustain hope and faith in those who were troubled by the profane tide that threatened them and to define a new role for the saints.[1]

This new perspective, signs of which can be seen even before the Restoration, saw the pulpit and the press being mobilized in different ways to meet new needs. The sense of participation in a millennial quest became muted as confidence in a Puritan transformation of England died. What hopes for such a change remained were of the more chiliastic variety, anticipating divine vengeance on a world that had gone astray. The saints had little role to play in such an apocalyptic climax to history. This made it more difficult for clergymen to draw attention to national covenants and communal responsibilities. Although individual reform was still—especially in New England—approached in terms of communal responsibilities, that orientation seemed less successful. Puritanism began to be seen less as a movement to transform the world than as a system to be preserved in its own right for the benefit it brought to individual Christians. And much of the literature of the latter seventeenth century was oriented toward individual moral striving.

Some changes in published Puritan writings were also influenced by external forces. In England censorship was reimposed, undoubtedly influencing some of the changes in literary efforts. The reintroduction of controls primarily affected English clergymen, whose primary outlets for publication were the printers of London, Cambridge, and Oxford. Much has been written about the Puritan authors' necessary adjustment to the experience of defeat. Milton, Bunyan, and others learned to use allegorical methods to make their points.

But the implications for colonists were also clear. John Eliot had prepared his visionary political tract, *The Christian Commonwealth*, in the late

1650s. In it he applauded the overthrow of the monarchy, supported the execution of Charles I, and called on the Puritan magistrates to move further toward the introduction of a biblically modeled society. But publication of the tract was delayed until 1660, just in time to catch the attention of the new king and his ministers. The Massachusetts authorities were forced to censure Eliot and burn copies of his book. It was clear that the publication of potentially revolutionary materials would not be tolerated in England or in the colonies.

John Davenport described the new situation in which the colonists found themselves in terms reminiscent of John Winthrop's explanation of what it had meant to be a Puritan in England in the 1620s. *The Saint's Anchor-Hold in All Storms and Tempests* was a series of sermons preached to his congregation in New Haven in the aftermath of the collapse of England's Puritan regime. He had himself assumed the risks of sheltering the regicides Edward Whalley and William Goffe when they sought a New England refuge from an English death sentence; Davenport argued that, despite the danger, it was the duty of the saints to "own the reproached and persecuted people and cause of Christ in suffering times." The plight of the regicides was clear proof of how the world had turned upside down. These men, who shortly before were among the most trusted lieutenants of England's Lord Protector, were now fugitives sheltering in the wilderness. The implications for all Puritans were clear. Once again, Davenport wrote, "reproachful titles [will be] put upon the people of God, whom profane men call fanatics." But the saints should not let themselves be moved by such attacks, for "he is a fool that will be laughed out of his coat, much more is he a fool, and a mad man, that will suffer himself to be laughed out of heaven, that will hazard the loss of his soul and salvation to free himself from the mocks and scoffs of a profane and sinful world" (*Anchor-Hold*, 228–29).

Some aspects of the Puritan message would have to be conveyed by indirect methods. One such method was to remember those who had fought the Lord's battles and to allow the recent past to serve as an inspiration for the present. Increasingly, in England and New England, efforts were made to memorialize the prominent Puritans of the Elizabethan and early Stuart periods, to preserve their memories, remember their sufferings, invoke their example, and sanctify their views. In England Samuel Clarke compiled a number of volumes along the lines of his *Lives of Thirty-Two English Divines Famous in their Generations for Learning and Piety* (1660). In America a comparable work would have to await Cotton Mather, but John Norton started a new genre with the publication of his funeral sermon commemorating John Cotton, *Abel Being Dead Yet Speaketh* (1658). John Davenport was said to have prepared a biography of Cotton that, never published, was subsequently lost. Samuel Whiting wrote a manuscript life of Cotton that survived but circulated only in manuscript in the colonial period. Much of this task of remembrance was undertaken by the first generation of New England–born clergy. Increase Mather memorialized his father in *The Life and Death of Mr. Richard Mather* (1670). William Hubbard remembered a friend in *A Funeral Discourse on Major Daniel Dennison* (1684). Urian Oakes published *An Elegy on the Rev. Thomas Shepard of Charlestown* (1677). Samuel Willard's sermons commemorating Thomas Savage, John Leverett, and John Hull were published, and such efforts became more common as the century advanced. It seemed as if a new generation needed to find its meaning by exploring its roots. In an age when fewer and fewer colonists felt the inner warmth of God's saving grace, more attention was directed to the outer manifestations of that grace in the lives of those who had clearly been God's elect.

This same interest is also evident in another new direction in the literature of the period, the appearance of works that focused on the struggles of the individual Christian in a hostile world rather than on the dawn of a new Christian era. Davenport anticipated a time of troubles in *The Saints Anchor-Hold*, which was published in London with the aid of the former New Englander William Hooke. English Puritans did not have long to wait to experience persecution, and the literature of the movement centered on that fact in the latter decades of the century. The works of Bunyan and Milton are the most significant examples, but similar messages were conveyed in clerical sermons and writings. Thomas Goodwin's *Patience and its Perfect Work* (1666) was prompted by the Great Fire of London but spoke more generally to the faithful. No longer was there hope of a Puritan England, and Goodwin sought to turn the attention of nonconformists from earthly success to the cultivation of a paradise within.

Suffering was part of the legacy Puritans had brought to New England. In the post-Restoration era the colonists learned of the plight of contemporary English nonconformists from correspondence with friends abroad, and also from those such as James Allen and Charles Morton who left England for colonial refuge in the post-Restoration era. But the colonists still held control over their society and hoped to keep it pure to pass on to their children. Many of the clergy still saw events such as fire, drought, and Indian war not primarily as tests of faith but as divine punishment for backsliding. Clerical authors directed considerable attention to attacking behavioral backsliding. Their sermons on such themes have evoked images of the biblical warnings of the prophet Jeremiah and thus have earned from historians the designation of "jeremiads." But such calls for repentance were not new to preachers like Davenport, who had said much the same thing to London listeners in the 1620s. Just as they had sought to awaken England to the need for repentance, so did they labor to stir reformation in New England. Somewhat in contradiction to this message, however, was a newer effort to accept and give positive meaning to suffering as the lot of the saint in this world. John Norton's *Three Choice and Profitable Sermons*, published in 1664, included a jeremiad-style sermon entitled "Sion the Out-cast Healed of Her Wounds" in which he informs his congregation that though they might be outcast for their sins, God will bring them the chance for repentance. But this message is followed by "The Believers Consolation, in the Remembrance of His Heavenly Mansion," in which Norton comforts his readers by urging them to hold on to God's promises to his saints despite the sufferings they might endure in this life for the truth. Like Job's, the faith of New England Puritans was to be tested. And in his last Thursday lecture John Allen similarly urged his congregation not to despair but to have faith in God's promises to them. The perseverance of the saints rather than their imminent triumph became a key theme in colonial sermons.

In many ways New England in the 1670s must have reminded some men, such as John Eliot, of England half a century earlier. A rising tide of luxury, disbelief, and self-seeking threatened the faith of the saints and the welfare of the society. The need to stand against adversity without surrender or compromise—a position epitomized by Milton's Samson—became a standard theme of late seventeenth–century Puritan writing. From this stance came what is referred to in England as the nonconformist conscience and what Americans call the Puritan conscience.

Related to these changes may have been a movement back toward a more evangelical style of preaching. Clergymen who had devoted many of their years in New England to nurturing a flock of saints began to take more seriously the need to strike the hearts of those awaiting God's grace. In the last of his sermons to be printed, Boston's John Wilson indicated in 1666 that he had "known New England about thirty-six years, and I never knew such a time as this is that we live in." Cotton Mather claimed that Wilson's New England preaching had been very methodical and, by inference, uninspiring. But in the closing years of his life the clergyman turned to a more lively pulpit style in which he sought to exhort his listeners. Much the same can be inferred from some of the recorded sermons of John Davenport.[2]

The Great Awakening of the eighteenth century was an expression of that tradition. The evangelical style of the revivalists harkened back to that of the seventeenth century's men of thunder, such as Rogers and Hooker. The reissuing in the 1730s and 1740s of seventeenth-century English and American devotional tracts and sermons on the nature of grace also testified to the relevance of the Puritan tradition. Shepard, Sibbes, and their contemporaries still had much to say to the generation of David Brainard and Jonathan Edwards. And even in our own time a publisher can find a market for pietistic works of the seventeenth-century divines, published as "Puritan Paperbacks"!

The Clergy and Their Writings

Among the ministers who sought to shape a new England were 49 English Puritans with Oxford or Cambridge training for the ministry who migrated to the New World before the outbreak of the English civil wars of the 1640s. Many of them are obscure, not even familiar to all colonial historians. I have attempted to provide a brief biographical sketch of each of them, through which it becomes clear that they had labored to reshape England before they embarked for the New World. I have also listed their published works and as an aid to scholars have indicated bibliographical references where possible. Not all early New England preachers are included. While recognizing their importance to the region's history, I have not included Stephen Bachiler, an Oxford graduate who, on his arrival in Massachusetts, was warned by the General Court to "forbear exercising his gifts as pastor," and Samuel Gorton and other preachers who were not university-trained.

Works that are listed in the *English Short Title Catalogues* are followed by the STC number. Works published prior to 1640 are listed in A. W. Pollard and G. W. Redgrave, *A Short Title Catalogue of Books Printed in England, Scotland and Ireland 1475–1640* (London, 1926); in the listing below the catalog number, these works are prefaced with the designation "PR." Works published between 1640 and 1700 are found in Donald Wing, *A Short Title Catalogue of Books Printed in England, Scotland and Ireland 1641–1700*, 3 vols., 2d ed. (New York, 1972–88), and are designated with a "W" followed by the catalog number. Books published in America that are listed in the Wing compilation are given the STC reference number. For books printed in America that are not found in the STC, I have listed their number from the *National Index of Early American Imprints through 1800*, 2 vols. (Worcester, Mass.; 1969), compiled by Clifford Shipton and James Mooney; the number is prefaced with the designation "NI." In some cases the authorship of a work is questionable, and I have exercised my best judgment as to whether to include it. I have not listed manuscript works, no matter how polished and publication-ready, but I have listed manuscripts that were published in later centuries and are hence readily available to students of the period. Place of publication is not given when it was London; all others are provided.

John Allen

John Allen, or Allin (c. 1596–1671) was the son of a Norfolk gentleman and attended the grammar school at North Walsham. He was admitted to Caius College, Cambridge, in 1612 and earned a B.A. degree in 1616 and an M.A. degree in 1619. He served as a curate in Denton and then in Wrentham but was forced from the ministry by Bishop Matthew Wren. He emigrated to New England and in 1638 helped found the church at Dedham, which he served as pastor. He assisted John Eliot in ministering to the Indians, was an overseer of Harvard, and joined with Thomas Shepard in defending the New England Way against English Presbyterian attacks.

Works:

A Defence of the Answer . . . Against the Reply . . . by Mr. John Ball, with Thomas
    Shepard (1648) [W: A1036]

Animadversions Upon the Antisynodalia Americana (Cambridge, Mass., 1664) [W:
    A1035]

The Spouse of Christ Coming Out of Affliction, Leaning Upon Her Beloved (Cambridge,
    Mass., 1672) [W: A1037]

"The Lord Jesus his Legacy of Peace" (1671), published in *Dedham Pulpit*, ed. E.
    Burgess (Boston, 1840)

Thomas Allen

Thomas Allen (c. 1609–73) was the son of a Norwich dyer. He studied at Caius College, Cambridge, where he received his B.A. degree in 1628 and M.A. degree in 1631. Following his ordination in 1634, he ministered to the Church of St. Edmund's in Norwich, but in 1638 he was suspended for refusing to read the Book of Sports, the royal authorization of Sunday activities that clergy were required to proclaim. He migrated to Massachusetts, settling first in Watertown and then accepting the call to be teacher of the Charlestown church. In 1651 he returned to England and became rector of St. George Tombland in Norwich. He was ejected in 1662 and died in 1673.

Works:

Chain of Scripture Chronology (1658) [W: A1047A]

The Way of the Spirit (1676) [W: A1047]

The Glory of Christ (Norwich, 1683) [W: A1046]

The Call of Christ unto Thirsty Sinners (Boston, 1705) [NI: 39418]

Peter Bulkeley

Peter Bulkeley (1583–1659) was born to a heritage of wealth and respect for learning. His father, Edward, came from a landed family and was a onetime fellow of St. John's College, Cambridge. Peter followed his father to St. John's, earning his B.A. degree in 1604 and his M.A. degree in 1608. He was appointed canon of Lichfield in 1609, and university preacher at Cambridge in the following year. When his father died, he inherited a large fortune and the rectory at Odell. He migrated to New England in 1635 and became one of the leading landowners as well as the pastor of the church at Concord, Massachusetts, where he served until his death in 1659. He was moderator of the 1637 Cambridge synod, which condemned the errors of the Hutchinsonians.

Works:

The Gospel Covenant (1646) [W: B5403]

Jonathan Burr

Jonathan Burr (1604–41) was the son of a Suffolk yeoman. After receiving his M.A. degree from Corpus Christi, Cambridge, in 1627, he preached at Horninger, near Bury, and then was rector of Rickinghall, Suffolk, until deprived of his living in 1639. He journeyed to New England and was admitted as a member of Richard Mather's Dorchester church. Burr was suspected of harboring some heretical familist views, but a conference of magistrates and ministers cleared him of the charge and he began to share ministerial duties with Mather. He died in 1641, before he could be formally ordained by the congregation.

Works: [None]

Charles Chauncy

Charles Chauncy (1592–1672) was perhaps the most distinguished scholar among the clerical immigrants. Like Bulkeley, Chauncy came from a landed family. He was born in Yardley-Bury, Hertfordshire, attended Westminster School, and matriculated at Trinity, Cambridge, in 1610. He received his B.A. degree in 1614, the M.A. degree in 1617, and his B.D. degree in 1624. He was also incorporated M.A. at Oxford in 1619. Chauncy served as a fellow of Trinity from 1614 to 1626; he was a Greek lecturer during the same period. On leaving the college, he served as vicar of St. Michael's, Cambridge, of Ware, in Hertfordshire, and of Marston, St. Lawrence. Suspended and imprisoned for nonconformity in 1637, he migrated to the New World and settled first at Plimoth and then in Scituate. In 1654 he was elected president of Harvard, a post he held until his death.

Works:

Retraction of Charles Chauncy (1641) [W: C3740]

The Doctrine of the Sacrament (1642) [W: C37376]
Gods Mercy Shewed to His People in Giving Them a Faithful Ministry and Schools of Learning (Cambridge, Mass., 1655) [W: C3738]
The Plain Doctrine of the Justification of Sinners (1659) [W: C3739]
Antisynodalia Scripte (1662) [W: C37377]

Ezekiel Cheever

Ezekiel Cheever (1615–1708) was perhaps the most noted schoolmaster of colonial America. Including him as a clergyman is indicative of how the two functions were often combined. Though he spent most of his career in the schoolroom, he was trained for the ministry and did preach on occasion. Cheever was born in London and educated at Emmanuel College, Cambridge. He came to Boston in 1637 but soon moved to the New Haven colony, where he opened a school in 1639. Among his best-known pupils were Michael Wigglesworth and Cotton Mather. He was censured by the church in 1649 when he accused the elders of usurping the authority of the congregation. Shortly thereafter he moved back to Massachusetts, teaching in Ipswich (1650–61), in Charlestown (1661–70), and at the Boston Latin School (1671–1708).

Works:

A Short Introduction to the Latin Tongue, for the Use of the Lower Forms in the Latin School (Boston, 1709) [NI: 1384]
Scripture Prophecies Explained (Boston, 1757) [NI: 7870]

Thomas Cobbett

Thomas Cobbett (1608–85) was born in Newbury, Berkshire, and attended Trinity College, Oxford, entering in 1627. According to Cotton Mather, Cobbett left Oxford during an outbreak of plague to study with William Twisse. After preaching briefly in Lincolnshire, he emigrated to Massachusetts in 1637. Cobbett served as teacher in Lynn, where he shared the pulpit with his friend from England, Samuel Whiting. In 1655 he succeeded Nathaniel Rogers as pastor in Ipswich, where he remained until his death.

Works:

A Just Vindication of the covenant (1648) [W: C4778]
The Civil Magistrates Power in matters of religion modestly debated (1653) [W:C4776]
A Practical Discourse of Prayer. Wherein is handled the Nature, the Duty, the Qualifications of Prayer (1654) [W: C4779]
A fruitful and full discourse (1656) [W: C4777]

John Cotton

John Cotton (1584–1652) was perhaps the most distinguished of all the English Puritan clergymen to migrate to New England. He was born in Derby, and educated at Emmanuel College, Cambridge (B.A., 1602; M.A., 1606; B.D., 1613). He was a fellow of Emmanuel from 1603 until 1612, at which time he accepted the post of rector of St. Botolph's Church in Boston, Lincolnshire. Cotton was an influential member of the clerical network and a noted mentor for younger clergymen until he departed for New England in 1633. He accepted the office of teacher in the First Church of Boston in Massachusetts. Though his reputation was tarnished somewhat by the preachings of his disciple Anne Hutchinson, Cotton regained his stature as the foremost colonial clergyman and one of the key spokesmen for the New England Way during the debates of the interregnum. He died in Boston in December 1652.

Works:

God's Promise to his Plantation (1630) [PR: 5854]

God's Mercy Mixed with His Justice (1641) [W: C6433]

The Way of Life for Gods Way and Course (1641) [W: C6470]

An Abstract, of The Laws of New England (1641) [W: C6408]

A Copy of a Letter of Mr. Cotton of Boston (1641) [W: C6422]

A Brief Exposition of the Whole Book of Canticles (1642) [W: C6410]

The True Constitution of a Particular Visible Church (1642) [W: C6468]

A Modest and Clear Answer to Mr. Balls Discourse of set formes of Prayer (1642) [W: C6444]

The Pouring Out of the Seven Vials; or, An Exposition of the Sixteenth Chapter of the Revelation, with an Application of it to our Times (1642) [W: C6449]

The Churches Resurrection, The True Constitution of a Particular Visible Church (1642) [W: C6419]

A Letter of Mr. John Cotton . . . to Mr. Williams (1643) [W: C6441]

Sixteen Questions of Serious and Necessary Consequence, Propounded unto Mr. John Cotton of Boston in New England, Together with his Answers to each Question (1644) [W: C6458]

The Keys of the Kingdom of Heaven (1644) [W: C6437]

The Way of the Churches of Christ in New England (1645) [W: C6471]

The Covenant of Gods Free Grace (1645) [W: C6423]

A Treatise of Mr. Cottons, Clearing certain Doubts concerning Predestination, Together with an Examination thereof: written by William Twisse (1646) [W: C6464]

The Controversy Concerning Liberty of Conscience in Matters of Religion (1646) [W: C6420]

A Conference Mr. John Cotton held at Boston (1646) [W: C6419]

Spiritual Milk for Babes in either England. Drawn Out of the Breasts of both Testaments for their souls nourishment (1646) [W: C6443]

The Bloody Tenent, Washed, and Made White in the Blood of the Lamb (1647) [W: C6409]

Singing of Psalms a Gospel Ordinance, with Thomas Shepard (1647) [W: C6456]

The Grounds and Ends of the Baptism of the Children of the Faithful (1647) [W: C6436]

The Way of the Congregational Churches Cleared (1648) [W: C6469]

Of the Holiness of Church Members (1650) [W: C6448]

Christ the Fountain of Life (1651) [W: C6417]

The New Covenant (1654) [W: C6447]

A Brief Exposition with Practical Observations upon the Whole Book of Ecclesiastes (1654) [W: C6413]

Certain Queries Tending to Accommodation and Communion of Presbyterian and Congregational Churches (1654) [W: C6416]

An Exposition upon the Thirteenth Chapter of Revelation (1655) [W: C6416]

A Brief Exposition with Practical Observations Upon the Whole Book of Canticles (1655) [W: C6412]

The Covenant of Grace (1655) [*A Treatise of the Covenant of Grace* (1659)] [W: C6425]

A Practical Commentary . . . upon the First Epistle of John (1656) [W: C6451]

A Defence of Mr. John Cotton from the Imputation of Self Contradiction Charged him by Mr. Dan: Cawdrey (Oxford, 1658) [W: C6427]

Some Treasure Fetched Out of Rubbish (1660) [W: C6459]

A Discourse about Civil Government in a New Plantation Whose Design is religion (Cambridge, Mass., 1663) [W: C6427]

A Treatise I. Of Faith. II. Twelve Fundamental Articles of Christian Religion. III. Doctrinal Conclusion. IV. Questions and Answers upon Church-government (Boston, 1713) [NI: 1604]

A Sermon . . . Delivered at Salem [1636] (Boston, 1713) [NI: 1603]

Manuscripts published in modern works:

"Mr. Cottons Rejoynder," reprinted in *The Antinomian Controversy, 1636–1638: A Documentary History*, ed. David D. Hall (Middletown, Conn., 1968).

"Sermon on Revelation 4:1–2," reprinted in George Selement, "John Cotton's Hidden Antinomianism," *New England Historical and Genealogical Register* 129 (1975).

"A Sermon on a Day of Publique Thanksgiving," reprinted in Francis J. Bremer, "In Defense of Regicide: John Cotton on the Execution of Charles I," *William and Mary Quarterly*, 3d. ser., 37 (1980).

"A Short discourse . . . touching the time when the Lords day beginneth," reprinted in Winton Solberg, "John Cotton's Treatise on the Duration of the Lord's Day," *Sibley's Heirs, Publications of the Colonial Society of Massachusetts* 59 (1982).

John Davenport

John Davenport (1597–1670) was the most active of the ministers who participated in the English reform movement of the 1620s. He was born in Coventry in April 1597. Davenport attended Merton College, Oxford, from 1613 to 1615 but left before completing his degree. After brief service as a private chaplain in the Durham region, he traveled to London and became curate at St. Lawrence Jewry in 1619. He attracted a following and in 1624 was chosen vicar of St. Stephen's Coleman Street. He completed his Oxford degree in 1625. Davenport worked with Richard Sibbes and other Puritan leaders in raising funds for refugees from the fighting in the Palatinate and was one of the organizers of the Feoffees for Impropriation. These activities and his increasing reluctance to cooperate with Laudian innovations led to his departure for the Netherlands in 1633. Like Hooker before him, he found his appointment in Rotterdam blocked by John Paget, after which he preached briefly in Amsterdam. In 1637 he journeyed to New England and participated in the defense of orthodoxy against Anne Hutchinson. Two years later he moved to New Haven, where he served as pastor and guiding spirit of the colony of the same name. In 1668 he accepted a call to the First Church of Boston, intending to use that pulpit to oppose the Half-Way Covenant. He died in 1670.

Works:

A Royal Edict for Military Exercises (1629) [PR: 6313]

A Just Complaint Against an Unjust Doer (Amsterdam, 1634) [PR: 6311]

A Protestation Made and Published Upon Occasion of a Pamphlet, Intitled a Just Complaint (Rotterdam, 1635) [PR: 6312]

An Apologetical Reply to . . . an Answer to the Unjust Complaint (Rotterdam, 1636) [PR: 6310]

A Profession of faith made at his admission into one of the Churches of God in New England (1642) [W: D364]

An Answer of the Elders of the Several Churches in New England unto Nine Positions Sent Over to Them (1643)

Church Government and Church Covenant Discussed in an Answer to the Elders (1643) [W: M1269]

The Knowledge of Christ Indispensably Required of All Men that Would Be Saved (1653) [W: D361]

A Catechism containing the chief heads . . . for . . . New Haven (1659) [W: D357]

The Saints Anchor-Hold, In All Storms and Tempests (1661) [W: D365]

Another Essay for Investigation of the Truth (Cambridge, Mass., 1663) [W: D356]

Gods Call to His People to Turn Unto Him (Cambridge, Mass., 1669) [W: D360]

A Sermon Preach'd at the Election of the Governor (Cambridge, Mass., 1670) [W: D367]

The Power of the Congregational Churches Asserted and Vindicated in Answer to a Treatise of Mr. J Paget (London, 1672) [W: D362]

Henry Dunster

Henry Dunster (1609–59) was born in a Lancashire village and educated at Magdalene College, Cambridge (B.A., 1631; M.A., 1634). He returned to his native Bury, where he was curate and schoolmaster from 1634 until he left for New England in 1640. Shortly after his arrival in Massachusetts he was named the first president of Harvard College, which he helped to shape after the colleges of Cambridge, England. He was forced to resign in 1654 when he refused to present his new son for baptism and would not agree to keep his Baptist principles to himself. He was allowed to migrate to Scituate, in the jurisdiction of Plimoth, where he ministered until his death in 1659.

Works:

Psalms, Hyms and Spiritual Songs (Cambridge, Mass., 1651) [W: B2470B]

Samuel Eaton

Samuel Eaton (1596-1665) was the third son of Richard Eaton, vicar of Great Budworth, Chesire. He attended Magdalene College, Cambridge, where he received his B.A. degree in 1625 and his M.A. degree three years later. In 1625 he was ordained deacon and priest at Peterborough. He was cited by the bishop of Chester for improperly administering communion and ejected from his living in Bromborough in 1632. He spent the following two years in the Netherlands and then returned to England, migrating to America in 1637 with his brother, Theophilus, and John Davenport. He settled in New Haven, where he had some differences with Davenport, and then returned to England to protect his estate in 1639. Remaining there as the civil wars swept the country, he became a leader of the Congregationalist effort in Chesire until his ejection in 1662.

Works:

A Defence of sundry positions and Scriptures alleged to justify the Congregational way (1645) [W: E118]

A just apology for the Church of Duckenfield (1647) [W: E122]

The mystery of God incarnate (1650) [W: E123]

A friendly debate on a weighty subject (1650) [W: E121]

The oath of allegiance (1650) [W: E124]

A vindication (1651) [W: E126]

The Quakers Confuted (1654) [W: E125]

John Eliot

John Eliot (1604–90) was born in Widford and raised in the nearby Essex village of Nazeing. He received his B.A. degree from Jesus College, Cambridge, in 1622 and returned to Essex, where he taught in a school maintained by Thomas Hooker in Little Baddow. When Hooker left England for the Netherlands, Eliot sailed for America. He preached briefly in the Boston church before accepting a call to Roxbury. There he became most noted for his missionary work among the Indians, translating the Scriptures and other religious material into the native language and establishing the convert communities known as praying towns. He lived to see King Philip's War and a growing English hostility to the tribes.

Works:

The Whole Book of Psalms, with R. Mather and T. Welde (Cambridge, Mass., 1640) [PR: 2738]

Tears of Repentance (1653) [W: E520]

A late and further manifestation of the progress of the Gospel among the Indians in New England (1655) [W: E517]

A further account of the progress of the Gospel amongst the Indians in New England (1659) [W: E510]

The Christian Commonwealth (1659) [W: E505]

The New Testament in the Indian Tongue (Cambridge, Mass., 1661) [W: B2757]

The Holy Bible [Indian language] (Cambridge, Mass., 1662) [W: B2747]

Communion of Churches (Cambridge, Mass., 1665) [W: E508]

The Indian Grammar begun (Cambridge, Mass., 1666) [W: E514]

The Indian Primer (Cambridge, Mass., 1669) [W: E 515]

A brief narrative of the progress of the Gospel among the Indians in New England in the year 1670 (1671) [W: E504]

Indian Dialogues (Cambridge, Mass., 1671) [W: E513]

The Logic Primer for the use of Indians (Cambridge, Mass., 1672) [W: E518]

The Harmony of the Gospels in English (Boston, 1678) [W: E512]

A Brief Answer to a . . . Book . . . against Infant Baptism (Boston, 1679) [W: E503]

Dying Speeches and Counsels of such Indians as died in the Lord (Cambridge, Mass., 1683) [W: E509]

Giles Firmin

Giles Firmin (1615–97) was born in Ipswich in 1615. He was the son of an apothecary and entered Emmanuel, Cambridge, in 1629 to study medicine. He was converted to Puritanism by the preaching of John Rogers of Dedham. Firmin left before taking a degree to accompany his father to New England in 1632, but he returned the following year to complete his medical studies in London.   He came back to Massachusetts in 1637 and was an opponent of the antinomians in the Boston church.   In 1638 he moved to Ipswich, where he practiced medicine.   He was the first colonist to prepare a skeleton and lecture on anatomy, but medicine was not profitable and he decided to study divinity.   He returned to England in 1644 and in 1648 was appointed rector of Shalford.   Firmin was an advocate of the New England Way and a member of an Essex association that included Ralph Josselin, but his Congregationalism did not prevent him from having close ties with moderate Presbyterians.   Ejected at the Restoration, he turned to the practice of medicine until the issuance of the Declaration of Indulgence provided him with an opportunity to be licensed as a Presbyterian minister.

Works:

A Serious Question Stated . . . Whether Ministers Of England are Bound by the Word of God to Baptize the Children of All Such Parents Which Sat they Believe in Jesus Christ (1651) [W: F965]

Separation Examined (1652) [W: F964]

A Sober Reply to the Sober Answer of Reverend Mr. Cawdrey, to a Serious Question Propounded (1653) [W: F966]

Stablishing against Shaking . . . in the Deluded People Called Quakers (1656) [W: F967]

Of Schism. Parochial Congregations in England and Ordination by Imposition of Hands (1658) [W: F958]

Tithes Vindicated (1659) [W: F968]

Presbyterial Ordination Vindicated (1660) [W: F961]

The Liturgical Considerator Considered; or, A Brief View of Dr. Gauden's Considerations Touching the Liturgy of the Church of England (1661) [W: F955]

The Real Christian; or, A Treatise of Effectual Calling (1670) [W: F963]

Meditations upon Mr. Baxter's Review of his Treatise on the Duty of Heavenly Meditations (1672) [W: F957]

The Questions between the Conformists and Nonconformists (1681) [W: F962]

The Plea of the Children (1683) [W: F960]

Scripture-warrant Sufficient Proof for Infant Baptism (1688) [W: F963A]

The Answer of Giles Firmin to the Vain and Unprofitable Question Put to Him . . . Whether the Greatest part of Dying Infants Shall Be Damned (1689) [W: F954A]

Weighty Questions Discussed (1692) [W: F969]

Some Remarks upon the Anabaptist Answer (1692) [W: F966A]

Hanergia a Brief Review of Mr. Davis's Vindication (1693) [W: F959]

John Fiske

John Fiske (1608–77) was another Suffolk Puritan. He was born in Elmham and attended Peterhouse College in Cambridge, graduating in 1628. After preaching for a few years, he appears to have turned to the practice of medicine to avoid persecution for nonconformity. In 1637 he journeyed to New England along with the Rev. John Allen. He farmed, practiced medicine, and taught school at Salem, occasionally assisting Hugh Peter in the pulpit. In 1644 he was called to be pastor of the congregation in Wenham, Massachusetts; he moved with the congregation to Chelmsford in 1655. Fiske authored a catechism that was published and kept a notebook and a commonplace book in which he wrote poetry.

Works:

The Watering of the Olive Plant in Christs Garden (Cambridge, Mass., 1657) [W: F1062]

The Notebook of the Reverend John Fiske, 1644–1675 (Boston, 1974)

Appendix of Catechism (Cambridge, Mass., 1668)

Francis Higginson

Francis Higginson (1586–1630) was one of the first ministers to come to the Bay colony. Higginson was born in Claybrooke, Leicestershire. He received his B.A. degree from Jesus College (1610) and M.A. degree (1613) from St. John's College, Cambridge. He then returned to Leicestershire to serve as curate in Claybrooke and then as lecturer at St. Nicholas (1617–27). He prepared a number of young men for Cambridge and was also active in aiding Palatine refugees. His nonconformity led to his deprivation and the initiation of proceedings against him in the Court of High Commission. Higginson accepted an appointment as one of the first clergymen sent to New England by the Massachusetts Bay Company, journeying to Salem in 1629 and becoming teacher to the church formed there. He died in August 1630.

Works:

New England's Plantation (1630) [PR: 13449]

Peter Hobart

Peter Hobart (1604–79) was born in Hingham, Norfolk. He was educated at the Free School in King's Lynn and then at Magdalene, Cambridge (B.A., 1626; M.A., 1629). He was curate at Haverhill until emigrating to New England in 1635. As pastor at Hingham, Massachussetts, he conducted church affairs according to his own

Presbyterian principles, which caused friction with some of his fellow ministers and with the colony magistrates. He died in 1679.

Works: [None]

William Hooke

William Hooke (1601–78) was born of comfortable parents in Hampshire and matriculated at Trinity, Oxford, in 1616. He received his B.A. degree in 1620 and his M.A. degree in 1623. After being ordained, he held clerical posts in Devon, where he was vicar at Axmouth. His preaching and nonconformity eventually forced him from the pulpit in 1637, at which time he migrated to New England. After having served as pastor of the church in Taunton, he moved to New Haven in 1644, where he joined his friend John Davenport in the pulpit. Hooke was related to Oliver Cromwell by his marriage to Jane Whalley, and he returned to Cromwell's England in 1656. The Lord Protector made him a household chaplain and master of the Savoy Hospital. He became a leader of the Congregational clergy in London and a participant in the assembly that prepared *The Savoy Declaration of Faith and Order*. He continued to preach in London after his ejection at the Restoration and was licensed under the Declaration of Indulgence in 1672. He retained a correspondence with New England friends such as John Davenport and with the exiled regicides Whalley and Goffe, to whom he was related by marriage. On his death, he was buried at Bunhill Fields.

Works:
New England's Tears for Old Englands Fears (1641) [W: H2624]
New Englands Sense of Old Englands and Irelands Sorrowes (1645) [W: H2623]
The privileges of the Saints (1673) [W: H2627]
A Short Discourse (1673) [W: H2629]
A Discourse Concerning the Witnesses (1681) [W: H2622]

Thomas Hooker

Thomas Hooker (1586–1647) was one of the clergymen whose departure to America attracted the most attention in English Puritan circles. He had been born in Marfield in July 1586. He attended Emmanuel, Cambridge, where he received his B.A. degree (1608) and his M.A. degree (1611). He served as a Dixie fellow and catechist at Emmanuel until 1618 and was a colleague of Cotton for much of that time. When he left Cambridge, he served as rector of Esher in Surrey and then went to St. Mary, Chelmsford in Essex as lecturer in 1626. There he became the center of a group of Puritan clergy in Essex that included Thomas Welde, Jeremiah Burroughes, John Eliot, and Thomas Shepard. In 1630 he journeyed to Rotterdam to accept a position in the English congregation, but a dispute with John Paget denied him that chance. In 1633 he traveled to New England, and after a brief stay in Newtown (later Cambridge), Massachusetts, he led the migration that founded the Connecticut colony in 1636. He served as pastor to the Hartford church until his death in 1647.

Works:

The Poor Doubting Christian (1629; 6th ed., 1641) {W: H2651B}
The Souls Preparation for Christ (1632) {PR: 13735}
The Souls Humiliation (1637) {W: 13728}
The Souls Ingrafting into Christ (1637) {PR: 13733}
The Souls Implantation (1637) {PR: 13731}
The Souls Effectual Calling to Christ (1637; reprinted as *The Souls Vocation*, 1638) {PR: 13739}
Four Godly and Learned Treatises (1638) {PR: 13725}
The Sinners Salvation (1638) {PR: 22578}
The Souls Exaltation (1638) {PR: 13727}
The Souls Possession of Christ (1638) {PR: 13734}
The Stay of the Faithful (1638) {PR: 23240}
Three Godly Sermons (1638) {PR: 13739}
The Unbelievers Preparing for Christ (1638) {PR: 13740}
The Christians Two Chief Lessons (1640) {PR: 13724}
The Pattern of Perfection (1640) {PR: 13726}
The Danger of Desertion (1641) {W: H2645}
The Faithful Covenanter (1644) {W: H2648}
The Saints Guide (1645) {W: H2655}
Heaven's Treasury Opened (1645) {W: H2650}
A Brief Exposition of the Lords Prayer (1645) {W: H2642}
An Exposition of the Principles of Religion (1645) {W: H2647}
A Survey of the Sum of Church Discipline (1648) {W: H2658}
The Covenant of Grace Opened (1649) {W: H2644}
The Saints Dignity and Duty (1651) {W: H2654}
The Application of Redemption, First Eight Books (1656) {W: H2639}
A Comment upon Christs Last Prayer (1656) {W: H2643}
The Application of Redemption, Ninth and Tenth Books (1657) {W: H2640}

Manuscripts published in modern editions:

"Abstracts of Two Sermons by Rev. Thomas Hooker from the Shorthand Notes of Mr. Henry Wolcott, *Collections of the Connecticut Historical Society* 1 (1860)

"Touching ye Crosse in ye Banners," *Proceedings of the Massachusetts Historical Society*, 3d. ser., 42 (1909)

"A Thomas Hooker Sermon of 1638," edited by Everett Emerson, *Resources for American Literary Study* 2 (1972)

"John Paget's XX Questions and Thomas Hooker's Answers," in *Thomas Hooker: Writings in England and Holland, 1626–1633*, ed. George H. Williams, Norman Petit, Winfried Herget, and Sargent Bush, Jr. (Cambridge, Mass., 1975)

Ephraim Huit

Ephraim Huit (?–1644) was minister in Wroxhall, Warwickshire, until deprived for nonconformity in 1638. He migrated to America and settled, as a colleague of John Warham, in Windsor, Connecticut.

Works:

The Prophecy of Daniel Explained (1643) [W: H3359]

John Knowles

John Knowles (c. 1606–85) was born in Lincolnshire and matriculated at Magdalene, Cambridge, in 1620. As an undergraduate, he shared chambers with Richard Vines. Knowles received his B.A. degree in 1624 and his M.A. degree in 1627 and was elected a fellow of St. Catherine's College. After he left Cambridge, he was lecturer at Colchester from 1635 to 1637 and then migrated to New England in 1639. He was copastor at Watertown with George Phillips. In 1651 he returned to England and was lecturer at Bristol Cathedral until he was ejected following the Restoration. He moved to London and ministered to a Congregational church there. He was recommended for the presidency of Harvard but declined to serve.

Works:

A Modest Plea for Private Mens Preaching (1648) [W: K730]

John Lothrop

John Lothrop (1584–1653) was born in Yorkshire and began his college studies at Oxford. He transferred to Cambridge, taking his B.A. degree from Queen's College in 1607 and his M.A. degree in 1609. He ministered to congregations in Kent and Hertsfordshire but then renounced his orders. He succeeded Henry Jacobs as pastor of a London independent congregation in 1624. Lothrop was arrested with other members of the congregation in 1632 and subsequently migrated to America. He ministered to churches in Scituate and Barnstable and died in 1653.

Works: [None]

Richard Mather

Richard Mather (1596–1669) was born of yeoman parents in Lancashire, attended the local grammar school, and taught school in Toxteth Park, near Liverpool, before proceeding to Brasenose College, Oxford, in 1618. He left Oxford without receiving a degree in order to be ordained and to minister to the people of Toxteth Park. Mather was deprived of his living for nonconformity in 1633 and in 1635 migrated to Massachusetts, where he soon accepted a call to minister to the congregation gathering in Dorchester. While not possessing the reputation of a Cotton or a Davenport, he became one of the pillars of the New England Congregational establishment, playing a key role in the authorship of the *Cambridge Platform* and proposing the Half-Way Covenant.

Works:

The Whole Book of Psalms, with J. Eliot and T. Welde (Cambridge, Mass., 1640) [PR: 2738]

An Apology of the Churches in New England for Church Government (1643) [W: M1267]

Church Government and Church Covenant Discussed . . . an Answer to Two and Thirty Questions (1643) [W: M1269]

A Modest and Brotherly Answer to Mr. Charles Herle, with William Tompson (1644) [W: M1274]

A Reply to Mr. Rutherford; or, A Defence of the Answer to Reverend Mr. Herles Book (1647) [W: M1275]

A Platform of Church Discipline (Cambridge, Mass., 1649) [W: P2396]

An Heart-Melting Exhortation Together with a Cordial Consolation, with William Tompson (1650) [W: M1273]

A Catechism; or, The Grounds and Principles of the Christian Religion (1650) [W: M1268]

The Sum of Certain Sermons Upon Genes: 15.6 (Cambridge, Mass., 1652) [W: M1276]

A Farewell-Exhortation to the Church and People of Dorchester (Cambridge, Mass., 1657) [W: M1272]

A Disputation Concerning Church-Members and Their Children (1659) [W: M1271A]

A Defence of the Answer and Arguments of the Synod Met at Boston in the Year 1662 (Cambridge, Mass., 1664) [W: M1271]

An Answer to Two Questions: Question I. Whether Does the Power of Church Government Belong to all the People, or to the Elders Alone? Question II. Whether Does Any Church Power, or Any Power of the Keys Belong to the People (Boston, 1712). [NI: 39554]

Samuel Newman

Samuel Newman (1600–1663) was born in Banbury, Oxfordshire. He matriculated at Magdalen College, Oxford, in 1616 and received his B.A. degree from St. Edmund Hall in 1620. After his ordination, he served in the ministry in Oxfordshire and elsewhere until 1635, when he decided to emigrate. He settled first in Weymouth, Massachusetts, and then in 1644 became the first pastor of the church at Rehoboth.

Works:

A Concordance to Holy Scriptures (1643) [1662 ed., W: S925]

John Norton

John Norton (1606–63) came from Stortford, Hertfordshire. He was tutored as a youth by Alexander Strange and entered Peterhouse College, Cambridge, at the age of 14, receiving his B.A. degree in 1623 and his M.A. degree in 1627. Forced to leave the university because of family financial troubles, he accepted a post as usher at the Stortford Grammar School and also served as the local curate. He was influenced by the preaching of Jeremiah Dyke and other local Puritans and turned down a church benefice to become chaplain to Sir William Masham of High Lever, Essex. In 1634 he joined Thomas Shepard in migrating to the New World. He took a lead in the opposition to Anne Hutchinson and in 1638 became teacher to the Ipswich church, whose pastor was Nathaniel Rogers. He succeeded John Cotton as teacher in the First Church of Boston in 1656. He also served as an overseer of Harvard, advised the magistrates on a number of occasions, and traveled to England as an agent of Massachusetts in 1662. He was noted for his strong opposition to the Quakers.

Works:

Responsio ad Totam Quaestionum (1648) [W: N1322]

A Brief and Excellent Treatise Containing the Doctrine of Godliness (1648) [W: N1315]

A Discussion of that Great Point in Divinity (1653) [W: N1317]

The Orthodox Evangelist (1654) [W: N1320]

Abel Being Dead Yet Speaketh (1658) [W: N1313]

The Heart of New England Rent at the Blasphemies of the Present Generation (Cambridge, Mass., 1659) [W: N1318]

A Brief Catechism (Cambridge, Mass., 1660) [NI: 63]

A Copy of the Letter Returned by the Ministers of New England to Mr. John Dury (Cambridge, Mass., 1664) [NI: 91]

Three Choice and Profitable Sermons (Cambridge, Mass., 1664) [W: N1324]

James Noyes

James Noyes (1608–56) was a cousin and colleague of Thomas Parker and shared the latter's Presbyterian principles. Noyes was the son of the Rev. William Noyes and nephew of the theologian Robert Parker. He was born in Wiltshire and studied at Brasenose College, Oxford. On leaving Oxford, he assisted Thomas Parker in the Free School in Newbury until both left for New England in 1634. The two ministered to the church in Newbury, Massachusetts.

Works:

The Temple Measured; or, A Brief Survey of the Temple Mystical (1647) [W: N1460]
Moses and Aaron; or, The Rights of Church and State (1661) [W: N1457]
A Short Catechism (Cambridge, Mass., 1661) [W: N1458]

Thomas Parker

Thomas Parker (1595–1677), the son of the Puritan divine and theologian Robert Parker (1564–1614), came from a distinguished clerical background. He studied first at Trinity College, Dublin, then at Oxford, the University of Leyden, and finally under his father's friend William Ames at the University of Franeker. He received his M.A. degree from Franeker in 1617. He returned to England, where he served as schoolmaster and assistant to the Rev. William Twisse, who was to preside over the Westminster Assembly. Parker emigrated to New England in 1634, settling a few years later in Newbury, Massachusetts, where he ministered until his death in 1677. His Congregational brethren pointed to their toleration of his Presbyterian views as proof that advocates of the two polities could coexist.

Works:

The True Copy of a Letter (1644) [W: P482]
The Visions and Prophecies of Daniel (1646) [W: P480]
Theses Theologicae de Traductione (1652) [W: P479]
Methodus Gratiae Divinae (1657) [W: P477]

Ralph Partridge

Ralph Partridge (1579–1658) was born in Kent in 1579. He studied at Cambridge, where he received his B.A. degree in 1600 and earned his M.A. degree from Trinity College in 1603. He was curate at Sutton-by-Dover, Kent, from 1619 to 1625. He emigrated to New England in 1636 and accepted an invitation to minister to the church at Duxbury, in the Plimoth colony, where he remained until his death in 1658. He was chosen, along with Richard Mather and John Cotton, to prepare the *Cambridge Platform* in 1648.

Works:
A Platform of Church Discipline, with others (Cambridge, Mass., 1649) [W: P2396]

Robert Peck

Robert Peck (1580–1658) was born in Beccles, Suffolk, and, like many of the Puritan clergy, attended Cambridge. He received his B.A. degree from St. Catherine's in 1599 and his M.A. degree from Magdalene in 1603. After he was ordained in 1605, he served as curate of Oulton and then as rector of Hingham, Norfolk, of which living he was deprived in 1638. He emigrated to Massachusetts and served as teacher of the church at Hingham. He returned to England in 1641 and in 1646 was restored to his former parish, where he ministered until his death.

Works: [None]

Hugh Peter

Hugh Peter (1598-1660) had the distinction of being the only clergyman executed as a regicide. Peter was born in Cornwall, the son of Flemish refugees from Antwerp. He was educated at Trinity College, Cambridge (B.A., 1618; M.A., 1622) and ordained in 1623. He was curate at Rayleigh, Essex, and then a lecturer at St. Sepulchre's in London. He was a friend of Richard Sibbes and John Davenport and a supporter of the Feoffees for Impropriation. After his license to preach was suspended in 1628, he stayed briefly at the University of Franeker in the Netherlands, where William Ames obtained a position for him. But in 1629 he was called to minister to an English congregation in Rotterdam, which he remodeled with a church covenant and strict membership requirements. Ames served briefly with him in Rotterdam in 1633, and John Davenport was his copastor in 1635. He migrated to Massachusetts in 1635 and succeeded Roger Williams as pastor of the Salem church. He returned to England as a colony agent in 1641 and remained there, defending New England interests, serving as an army chaplain, preaching to Parliament, and representing the government abroad. His identification with the Puritan regime was such that he was excluded from pardon at the Restoration and executed as a regicide in October 1660.

Works:
Milk for Babes and Meat for Men (Rotterdam, 1630; Eng. ed., 1641) [W: P1712]
Digitus Dei; or, Good News from Holland (Rotterdam, 1631) [PR: 19066]
A True Relation of . . . a Voyage for Ireland (1642) [W: P1722]
"Life of Colonel Harwood," in *The Advice of Sir Ed Harwood* (1642) [W: H1096]

Mr. Peters Report from the Army (1645) [W: P1716]
Mr. Peters Report from Bristol (1645) [W: P1715]
A Copy of . . . Mr. Peters Report to the House of Commons (1645) [W: P1718]
The Full and Last Relation of . . . Basing House (1645) [W: P1702]
Mr. Peters Message (1646) [W: P1711]
God's doings and man's duty, opened in a sermon preached before the House of Commons and Assembly of Divines (1646) [W: P1703]
Mr. Peters last report of the English wars (1646) [W: P1707]
A word for the Army and two words for the Kingdom (1647) [W: P1726]
A Letter from Ireland (1649) [W: P1709]
Good work for a good magistrate (1651) [W: P1706]
Aeternitati Sacrum (1651) [W: P1694]
Some notes of a sermon . . . preached . . . after his condemnation (1660) [W: P1717]
A dying father's last legacy to an only child (1660) [W: P1697]
The Case of Mr. Hugh Peter (1660) [W: P1695]

George Phillips

George Phillips (1593–1644) was another East Anglian. He studied at Tivetshall School and then was admitted to Caius College, Cambridge, in 1610. He received his B.A. degree in 1614 and his M.A. degree in 1617. Phillips served as curate at Boxted, Essex, but lived in Wrentham. He emigrated with the Winthrop fleet in 1630 and became the first pastor at Watertown, serving there until his death in 1644.

Works:
Reply to the confutation of some grounds of infant baptism (1645) [W: P2026]

John Phillips

John Phillips (1585–1660) came from the same Suffolk background that produced John Winthrop and so many other members of the Great Migration. He received his degrees from Emmanuel College, Cambridge (B.A., 1604; M.A., 1607) and then served as rector of Wrentham, Suffolk. He married the sister of William Ames. Phillips was deprived of his living in 1638 and migrated to Massachusetts. In 1641 he returned to England and recovered his former rectory. He reorganized the Wrentham church on Congregational principles. He died in 1660.

Works: [None]

Abraham Pierson

Abraham Pierson (?–1678) came from Yorkshire to Cambridge in 1629 and received his B.A. degree from Trinity College in 1632. He migrated to New England in 1639 and accepted a call to the church in Southampton, Long Island, which was part of the New Haven colony.

In 1644 he crossed the sound to minister to the church at Branford, Connecticut. He devoted great effort to conversion of the Indians, preaching to them in their own language. Distressed by the 1662 union of Connecticut and New Haven, he was among those who left New England to found New Ark in what became New Jersey.

Works:

Some Help for the Indians in New Haven (Cambridge, Mass., 1658) [W: P2213]

Ezekiel Rogers

Ezekiel Rogers (1590–1660) was the son of Richard Rogers, the lecturer at Wethersfield, Essex. Ezekiel took his B.A. degree from Christ's College, Cambridge, in 1605 and his M.A. degree three years later. He was chaplain to Sir Francis Barrington of Broad Oak, Essex, and in 1621 became rector of Rowley St. Peter in Yorkshire. In 1638 he resigned his living and emigrated to Massachusetts rather than read the Book of Sports. He founded the town of Rowley and became its first pastor, serving there until his death in 1660.

Works:

The Chief Grounds of a Christian Religion (1642) [W: R1800]

Nathaniel Rogers

Nathaniel Rogers (1598–1655), like Thomas Parker, came from a distinguished clerical background. He was the son of Dedham's lecturer, John Rogers, and the nephew of Richard Rogers. Nathaniel was admitted to Emmanuel College, Cambridge, in 1614 and received his B.A. degree in 1618 and his M.A. degree in 1621. After his ordination, he served as curate at Bocking, Essex, and in 1630 he became rector at Assington, Suffolk. Rogers migrated to Massachusetts in 1636 and succeeded Nathaniel Ward as pastor of the Ipswich church in 1638. John Norton was his colleague.

Works:

A Letter Discovering the Cause of Gods Continuing Wrath (1643) [W: R1821]

Thomas Shepard

Thomas Shepard (1605–49) was born in Northamptonshire to a grocer's apprentice and his wife. He was orphaned early in life and entered Emmanuel College, Cambridge, as a pensioner. He received his B.A. and M.A. degrees and was ordained in 1627. Shepard was silenced by Archbishop Laud in 1630 but preached underground for the next few years until moving to Massachusetts in 1635. He was chosen pastor of the Newtown (soon Cambridge) church and became closely involved as well with neighboring Harvard College after its formation. He was involved in the refutation of Anne Hutchinson's views and later became involved in the defense of the New England Way against its English Presbyterian critics.

Works:

The Sincere Convert (1640) [W: S3118]

The Saints Jewell (1642) [NI: 39473]

New Englands Lamentations for Old England Errors (1645) [W: S3113]

The Sound Believer; or, A Treatise of Evangelical Conversion (1645) [W: S3132]

Certain Select cases Resolved (1648) [W: S3103]

The Clear Sunshine of the Gospel Breaking on the Indians (1648) [W: S3109]

A Defense of the Answer . . . Against the Reply . . . by Mr John Ball, with John Allen (1648) [W: A1036]

Theses Sabbaticae (1649) [W: S3144]

A Treatise of Ineffectual Hearing of the Word (1652)

Subjection to Christ in all His Ordinances (1652) [W: S3141]

The First Principles of the Oracles of God (1648) [W: S3112]

The Parable of the Ten Virgins (1660) [W: S3114]

The Church Membership of Children and their Right to Baptism (Cambridge, Mass., 1663) [W: S3108]

Wine for Gospel Wantons (Cambridge, Mass., 1668) [W: S3150]

Two Questions, viz. I. Whether an Account of the Work of Grace is to be Required of Those that are admitted to Full Communion? II. Whether the Whole Church is to be Judged Thereof? (Boston, 1697) [W: S3149]

Manuscripts published in modern editions:

"Journal and Autobiography," published as *God's Plot, The Paradoxes of Puritan Piety: Being the Autobiography and Journal of Thomas Shepard*, ed. Michael McGiffert (Amherst, Mass., 1972)

John Sherman

John Sherman (1613–85) was born in Dedham, Essex, and was led to Puritanism by the preaching of John Rogers. He matriculated at Emmanuel College, Cambridge, but failed to take a degree because he would not take the newly instituted oath requiring subscription to the practices of the Church. He came to New England in 1634. After a brief stay as an assistant to George Phillips at Watertown, Sherman went to the New Haven colony, where he preached in a number of towns without accepting a ministerial position. He eventually succeeded Phillips at Watertown, remaining there from 1647 until his death in 1685. He was one of the moderators of the Reforming Synod of 1679.

Works:
An Almanac for 1674 (Cambridge, Mass., 1674) [NI: 196]
An Almanac for 1676 (Cambridge, Mass., 1676) [NI: 223]
An Almanac for 1677 (Cambridge, Mass., 1677) [NI: 241]

Samuel Skelton

Samuel Skelton (1593–1634) was born in Lincolnshire in 1593, received his B.A. degree in 1611 and M.A. degree in 1615 from Clare Hall, Cambridge, and then was named rector of Sempringham. He probably also served for a time as chaplain to the Earl of Lincoln and was involved with those who organized the Massachusetts Bay Company. He was one of the first ministers sent to the New World by the company, serving with Francis Higginson in the church at Salem until his death in 1634.

Works: [None]

Samuel Stone

Samuel Stone (1602–63) was born in Hertford and educated at Emmanuel College, Cambridge, where he first encountered Thomas Hooker. He was appointed a curate at Stisted, Essex, in 1627 but was suspended for nonconformity three years later. He migrated to New England and joined Hooker in ministering to the Newtown, Massachusetts, congregation. Together with Hooker, he moved to Connecticut in 1636. He served as a chaplain in the 1637 war against the Pequots. Following Hooker's death, he ministered to the Hartford church as its pastor until his own death in 1663.

Works:
A Congregational Church is a Catholic Visible Church (1652) [W: S5734]
A Short Catechism (Boston, 1699) [W: S5737]

William Tompson

William Tompson (1598–1666) was born in Lancashire and educated at Brasenose College, Oxford. He received his B.A. degree in 1622. In Lancashire his clerical friends included both Richard Mather and Charles Herle. He migrated to Massachusetts in 1637, preached for a time in Maine, and then became minister at Braintree. He served as one of the Massachusetts missionaries to Virginia from 1642 to 1643, returning then to Massachusetts. According to Cotton Mather, he suffered from depression, which kept him from exercising his preaching gifts for a number of years.

Works:

A Modest & Brotherly Answer to Mr. Charles Herle, with Richard Mather (1644)
   [W: M1274]
An Heart-Melting Exhortation Together with a Cordial Consolation, with Richard
   Mather (1650) [W: M1273]

Nathaniel Ward

Nathaniel Ward (1578–1652) was the oldest of the clerical immigrants.
He was the son of John Ward, a Puritan preacher of Bury St. Edmund in
Suffolk. Born in Haverhill, Ward had studied at Emmanuel College,
Cambridge. After receiving his M.A. degree in 1603, he practiced law,
later traveling to the Continent, where he was influenced by the
Calvinist clergyman David Pareus and was ordained into the ministry in
1618. He served an English congregation in Ebling until 1624, when he
returned to England and accepted a curacy at St. James's Picadilly. In
1628 Ward was appointed rector of Stondon-Massey in Essex, a post he
held until silenced by Archbishop Laud in 1633. Migrating to
Massachusetts, he served briefly as copastor in Ipswich, then retired from
the ministry. His legal background made him an important figure in
compiling the Massachusetts *Body of Liberties* (1641). He wrote *The
Simple Cobbler of Agawam* shortly before returning to England in 1647.
Ward preached before Parliament and became an outspoken enemy of
sectarianism, identifying with the Presbyterian concern for order. He
returned to the ministry in 1648.
   Works:
The Simple Cobbler of Agawam (1647) [W: W786]
A Religious Retreat Sounded to a Religious Army (1647) [W: W782]
A Word to Mr. Peters and Two Words to the Parliament and Kingdom (1647) [W:
   W792]
*A Sermon Preached before the Honorable House of Commons at their Monthly Fast June
   30, 1647* (1647) [W: W784]
To the High and Honorable Parliament of England (1648) [W: W791]

John Warham

John Warham (?–1670) served in the ministry in Exeter and then was
chosen pastor of a congregation gathered in Plymouth, England, for the
purpose of traveling together to America. It is not clear that he actually
had university training. The group settled in Dorchester, Massachusetts,
but in 1636 joined the migration to Connecticut, settling in the town of
Windsor. Warham served there until his death in 1670.
   Works: [None]

Thomas Welde

Thomas Welde (1595–1661) was born in Sudbury, Suffolk. He was the fourth son of a linen draper but attended Cambridge, matriculating as a pensioner at Trinity College in 1611. He received his B.A. degree in 1614 and his M.A. degree in 1618 and was ordained to the ministry. He was vicar of Haverhill, Suffolk, and then Terling in Essex. While at Terling, he was closely associated with Thomas Hooker. Deprived of his living for nonconformity in 1631, he emigrated to Massachusetts and became the first pastor of the Roxbury congregation, where he was associated with his Essex friend John Eliot. Anne Hutchinson was kept a prisoner in his house prior to her banishment. In 1641 he was sent along with Hugh Peter to represent the Bay colony in England. He promoted the cause of the colony, and of Harvard, and became a defender of the Congregational system. After serving in other ministerial posts, he was installed at St. Mary's, Gateshead, Durham, where he created controversy by his introduction of New England practices. He joined with other orthodox clergy of the region in opposition to the Quakers. He died shortly after the Restoration.

Works:

The Whole Book of Psalms, with J. Eliot and R. Mather (Cambridge, Mass., 1640) [PR: 2738]

New Englands First Fruits (1643) [W: E519]

An Answer to W.R. his narration (1644) [W: W1262]

A Brief Narration of the Practices of the Churches of New England (1645) [W: W1263]

A False Jew (1653) [W: W1266]

The Perfect Pharisee under Monkish holiness (1654) [W: W1268A]

A Further Discovery of that Generation of Men Called Quakers (1654) [W: W1268]

John Wheelwright

John Wheelwright (1592–1679) became the only clergyman punished for involvement in the antinomian controversy in Massachusetts. He was the son of a Lincolnshire yeoman and was educated at Sidney Sussex College, Cambridge (B.A., 1615; M.A., 1618). Wheelwright was vicar at Bilsby, Lincolnshire, from 1623 to 1632 and then preached at Belleau, where Henry Vane had a seat. He emigrated to Massachusetts in 1636 and was exiled a year later for his support of his sister-in-law Anne Hutchinson. He journeyed to England in 1656, but after the Restoration he returned to Massachusetts. His sentence of banishment had been lifted, and he ministered in New England until his death in 1679.

Works:

Mercurius Americanus, Mr. Welds {sic} his Antitype; or, Massachusetts great Apology examined (1645) [W: W1605]
A Brief and Plain Apology (1658) [W: W1604]
A Sermon Preached at Boston in New England upon a Fast Day, the 19th of January 1636–37 (Cambridge, Mass., 1867)

Henry Whitfield

Henry Whitfield (c. 1591–1657) was the son of an attorney in Surrey. He matriculated at New College, Oxford, in 1610, but there is no record of his receiving a degree. Cotton Mather states that he studied at the Inns of Court after leaving Oxford. Whitfield was ordained and installed as rector of Ockley, Surrey, where he ministered from 1618 to 1638. He left for New England the following year and became one of the founders of Guilford, Connecticut, as well as pastor of the church there. He returned to England in 1650 and served in the ministry at Winchester. In England he became one of the leading supporters of John Eliot's missionary work.

Works:
Some help to stir up Christian duties (1636) [PR: 25410]
The Light Appearing (1651) [W: W1999]
Strength Out of Weakness (1652) [W: W1999]

Samuel Whiting

Samuel Whiting (1597–1679) was a close friend and associate of John Cotton. He was born in Boston, where his father was mayor in 1600 and 1608. He received his B.A. degree in 1616 and his M.A. degree in 1620 from Emmanuel College, Cambridge, earning a reputation as a proficient Hebrew scholar. Whiting was prosecuted for nonconformity at his first clerical living in Lynn Regis, and again in Skirbeck. In 1636 he migrated to New England, along with his second wife, the sister of Oliver St. John, who would be one of the leaders of the Long Parliament. Whiting evidently did not take part in the synod of 1637, perhaps because he was a friend of John Wheelwright, with whom he had journeyed to Massachusetts. In 1654 he was named an overseer of Harvard. He preached an artillery sermon in 1660 and presided over the Synod of 1662, which endorsed the Half-Way Covenant.

Works:
Oratio, Quam Comitiis Cantabrigiensibus Americanis Peroavit (Cambridge, Mass., 1649) [W: W2024]
A Discourse of the Last Judgement (Cambridge, Mass., 1664) [W: W2023]
Abraham's Humble Intercession for Sodom (Cambridge, Mass., 1666) [W: W2022]

Roger Williams

Roger Williams (1603–83) was born in London, the son of a merchant tailor. The jurist Sir Edward Coke recognized the talent of the young Williams and sponsored him at Charterhouse School and Pembroke Hall, Cambridge (B.A., 1627). Williams became chaplain to Sir William Masham in 1629 and made the acquaintance of a number of the future leaders of English and American Puritanism. He migrated to New England in 1630 and soon showed Separatist leanings, which eventually caused his expulsion from the ministry at Salem and banishment from Massachusetts in 1635. He settled along Narragansett Bay, where he founded the town of Providence. In 1643 he journeyed to England to gain a charter to protect Providence and the other Rhode Island settlements from incursions by their neighbor colonies. There he became involved in the English debate over religious toleration. On his return to New England he continued to defend his colony and his views against critics on all sides.

Works:

A Key into the Language of America (1643) [W: W2766]

The Bloody Tenent of Persecution, for cause of Conscience, in a Conference between Truth and Peace (1644) [W: W2758]

Mr. Cottons Letter Lately Printed, Examined and Answered (1644) [W: W2767]

Queries of Highest Consideration, Proposed to the five Holland Ministers (1644) [W: W2770]

Christenings Make Not Christians (1645) [W: W2761]

The Bloody Tenent Yet More Bloody (1652) [W: W2760]

Experiments of Spiritual Life (1652) [W: W2762]

The Hireling Ministry None of Christs (1652) [W: W2765]

The Fourth Paper Presented by Major Butler (1652) [W: W2763]

The Examiner Defended (1652) [W: E3732]

George Fox Digg'd Out of his Burrowes (Boston, 1676) [W: W2764]

An answer to a letter sent from Mr. Coddington (Boston, 1678) [W: W2757]

John Wilson

John Wilson (1588–1667) was born into the English establishment. His father was a canon at Windsor, and his mother was a niece of Archbishop Edmund Grindal. He was educated at Eton and then proceeded to King's College, Cambridge, where he took his B.A. degree (1610) and his M.A. degree (1613). At Cambridge he was converted to Puritanism and consequently lost his chance at preferment in the Church of England. He emigrated to New England in 1630 from Sudbury, where he had lectured for over a dozen years. He became the pastor of the First Church of Boston, with John Cotton as his colleague. Wilson was the primary target of Anne Hutchinson and her supporters in the events leading up to the antinomian controversy. In the later decades of his life he was a strong opponent of the Quaker incursion into the Bay colony.

Works:

Some Helps to Faith (1624) [PR: 25769]

A Song; or, Story, For the Lasting Remembrance of divers famous works, which God hath done in our time (1626) [PR: 22922]; later published as *A Song of Deliverance for the Lasting Remembrance of Gods Wonderful Works* (Boston, 1680) [W: W2878]

Zacheus Converted; or, The Rich Publicans Repentance (1631) [PR: 25770]

The Day-Breaking, if not the Sun-Rising of the Gospel with the Indians in New England (1647) [W: S3110]

A Copy of Verses Made (Cambridge, Mass., 1658) [W: W2896]

A Seasonable Watch-Word unto Christians against the Dreams and Dreamers of This Generation (Cambridge, Mass., 1677) [W: W2897]

Benjamin Woodbridge

Benjamin Woodbridge (1622–84) was the youngest of those educated in England to arrive in New England before the outbreak of the civil wars. He was born in Wiltshire and matriculated at Magdalen College, Oxford, in 1638. Two years later he left the university and migrated to Massachusetts to join his brother John and his uncle, Thomas Parker, in Newbury. He actually finished his studies at Harvard and became the college's first graduate in 1642. In 1647 he and his brother returned to England, carrying with them the manuscript of their sister-in-law Anne Bradstreet's *The Tenth Muse Lately Sprung Up in America* (1650). Woodbridge wrote poetry himself, and his verses showed a strong transatlantic viewpoint. Though he had arrived in New England after the Hutchinsonian controversy, his sermons in England revealed a concern with that New England heresy. A Presbyterian who had sympathies with the Congregationalists, he was ejected from his Newbury living at the Restoration. Woodbridge allowed himself to be ordained in the Church of England and was tempted to conform, but did not. He was licensed under the Declaration of Indulgence in 1672 and preached until his death in 1684.

Works:

Church Members set in Joynt; or, A Discovery of the Unwarrantable and Disorderly Practice of Private Christians in Usurping the Peculiar Office and Work of Christs Own Pastors, Namely Public Preaching (1648) [W: W3423]

Justification by Faith; or, A Confutation of that Antinomian Error, That Justification is Before Faith (1652) [W: W3424]
The Method of Grace in the Justification of Sinners (1656) [W: W3426]

Notes and References

Introduction

1. Thomas Hooker, *The Application of Redemption, First Eight Books* (London, 1656), 208.

Chapter One

1. Thomas Hooker, *A Survey of the Sum of Church Discipline* (London, 1648), sig A4v, hereafter cited in the text as *Survey*.

2. The phrase is from Diarmaid MacCullouch, *The Later Reformation in England, 1547–1603* (London, 1990), as part of the title for chap. 3. My discussion of the English religious scene is based in part on this work, as well as on Patrick Collinson's *The Religion of Protestants* (Oxford, 1983), *The Elizabethan Puritan Movement* (London, 1967), and *Godly People* (London, 1983); Peter Lake's *Moderate Puritans and the Elizabethan Church* (Cambridge, Eng., 1983); and Nicholas Tyacke's *Anti-Calvinists: The Rise of English Arminianism* (Oxford, 1987). Different views on the nature of English Puritans are to be found in Peter White, *Predestination, Policy and Polemic* (Cambridge, Eng., 1992) and Julian Davies, *The Caroline Captivity of the Church* (Cambridge, Eng., 1992). An extraordinary new study of the transformation of English lay piety during the Reformation era is Eamon Duffy's *The Stripping of the Altars* (New Haven, Conn., 1992).

3. Thomas Shepard, "Autobiography," in Michael McGiffert, ed., *God's Plot, The Paradoxes of Puritan Piety: Being the Autobiography and Journal of Thomas Shepard* (Amherst, Mass., 1972), 37.

4. Michael McGiffert, ed., *God's Plot, The Paradoxes of Puritan Piety: Being the Autobiography and Journal of Thomas Shepard* (Amherst, Mass., 1972).

5. For a discussion of Puritan theology, see the works cited in n. 2 and also R. T. Kendall, *Calvin and English Calvinists* (Oxford, 1979), and John Coolidge, *The Pauline Renaissance in England* (Oxford, 1970).

6. Patrick Collinson, *The Birthpangs of Protestant England* (New York, 1988), 99.

7. Margaret Spufford, *Small Books and Pleasant Histories: Popular Fiction and Its Readership in Seventeenth-Century England* (London, 1981), 9–10, hereafter cited in the text.

8. Tessa Watt, *Cheap Print and Popular Piety, 1550–1640* (Cambridge, Eng., 1991). For the place of the Bible in this literature, see Christopher Hill, *The English Bible and the Seventeenth-Century Revolution* (London, 1993).

9.   See Keith Thomas, *Religion and the Decline of Magic* (London, 1971). For a discussion of Marlow's *Doctor Faustus* that emphasizes the play's Calvinistic assumptions, see John Stachniewski, *The Persecutory Imagination: English Puritanism and the Literature of Despair* (Oxford, 1991), chap. 7.

10.   John Winthrop, "Religious Experience," *Winthrop Papers*, 6 vols., ongoing (Boston, 1927–), 1:196.

11.   For discussion of anti-Calvinism and the Laudian initiatives, see the works cited in n. 2 and also Kenneth Fincham, *Prelate as Pastor: The Episcopate of James I* (Oxford, 1990), hereafter cited in the text.

12.   Nicholas Tyacke has persuasively treated the theological innovations pursued by these English proto-Arminians. Other scholars, such as Peter Lake and Kenneth Fincham, have added to the picture by showing the connections between this anti-Calvinist theology and the new emphasis such clergymen placed on liturgical ceremonies and the sacramental rituals as means of grace.

13.   Thomas Goodwin, quoted in Hugh Kearney, *Scholars and Gentlemen* (Ithaca, N.Y., 1970), 94–95.

14.   The connections formed at Cambridge between Puritan clergymen and the impact of those friendships on the development of seventeenth-century Puritanism are explored in my forthcoming *Congregational Communion: Clerical Friendship in the Anglo-American Puritan Community, 1610–1692*, hereafter cited in the text.

15.   This and the following paragraph are based on Francis J. Bremer, "To Live Exemplary Lives," *The Seventeenth Century* 7 (1992): 27–39.

16.   Edward Johnson, *The Wonder-Working Providence of Sions Saviour in New England*, (165) ed. J. Franklin Jameson (New York, 1959), 49; Peter Bulkeley, *The Gospel Covenant* (London, 1646), 15; John Norton, *The Heart of New England Rent at the Blasphemies of the Present Generation* (Cambridge, Mass., 1659), 78; John Davenport quoted in Harry S. Stout, *The New England Soul* (New York, 1986), 62, hereafter cited in the text as Davenport in Stout.

17.   For a more detailed study of the relationship between New England and English Puritans, from the civil wars to the Glorious Revolution, see Francis J. Bremer, *Puritan Crisis: New England and the English Civil Wars* (New York, 1989), and *Congregational Communion*.

Chapter Two

1.   Thomas Hooker, *The Christians Two Chief Lessons* (London, 1640), 203; Arthur Dent, *Pastime for Parents* (London, 1606), unpaginated.

2.   Thomas Brooks to Richard Baxter, 24 December 1657, in N. H. Keeble and Geoffrey Nuttall, eds., *Calendar of the Correspondence of Richard Baxter, Vol. 1: 1638–1660* (Oxford, 1990), 284–85, hereafter cited in the text as *Calendar 1*; William Perkins, *The Works of William Perkins*, 3 vols. (London, 1626–31), 3:431, hereafter cited in text as *Perkins Works*.

3.   See John Morgan, *Godly Learning: Puritan Attitudes toward Reason, Learning, and Education, 1560–1640* (Cambridge, Eng., 1986), chap. 6.

4.   David Hall (*Worlds of Wonder, Days of Judgement* [New York, 1987], hereafter cited in the text) has discussed another difficulty that Puritan preachers may have faced in dealing with an audience. Looking at clergymen of the next generation, such as Increase Mather, he detects a frustration with their congregations' lower educational level, which inhibited them from displaying their own learning either in sermons or in print. "Who would buy their books," Hall asks, "if they diverged into 'Scholastiall Argumentations'?" (67). I do not find that sort of tension in the clergy of the first generation, who, as we will see, took it as a challenge to use their academic knowledge without flaunting it.

5.   Christopher Hill, "Censorship and English Literature," *The Collected Essays of Christopher Hill*, vol. 1 (Amherst, Mass., 1985), chap. 2; see also N. H. Keeble, *Literary Culture of Nonconformity in Later Seventeenth-Century England* (Athens, Ga.; 1987), hereafter cited in the text. The subject of the underground press is especially well dealt with in Stephen Foster's *Notes from the Caroline Underground: Alexander Leighton, the Puritan Triumvirate, and the Laudian Reaction to Nonconformity*, Studies in British History and Culture 6 (Hamden, Conn., 1978).

6.   John Cotton, *A Treatise of the Covenant of Grace* (London, 1659) [*The Covenant of Grace* (1655)], epistle, hereafter cited in the text as *Covenant of Grace*; George H. Williams, Norman Petit, Winfried Herget, and Sargent Bush, Jr., eds., *Thomas Hooker, Writings in England and Holland, 1626–1633* (Cambridge, Mass., 1975), 239 n. 88, hereafter cited in the text as *Hooker Writings*; Lewis Baylie, *The Practice of Piety* (London, 1631), 476.

7.   Keeble refers to the followers of Grew in *Literary Culture*, 78. David Cressy (*Literacy and the Social Order* [Cambridge, Eng., 1980], 5–6) tells how Oliver Heywood took notes on sermons for his mother when he was young. His father instructed him, when Oliver went to Cambridge, to take notes on the sermons he heard there and send them to his mother. Puritan clergymen favored the appearance of an extemporaneous delivery. Though some wrote out sermons beforehand, most only prepared notes and when urged to publish the sermon had to reconstruct it from those notes.

8.   Morton's manuscript does not survive but is mentioned by Keeble in *Literary Culture*; Keeble also points out that Milton's *De Doctrina Christiana* [circulated in manuscript, not published until 1825] is "the most celebrated, but by no means the only example of a substantial work written up in a fair copy but never submitted for licensing or delivered to the press" (110).

9.   Richard Baxter, *A Christian Directory* (London, 1673), 60.

10.   Thomas Bedford to Richard Baxter, 8 March 1651, *Calendar 1*, 65; Thomas Gataker to Richard Baxter, 1 March 1654, *Calendar 1*, 129.

11.   Richard Baxter, "To the Reader," in Richard Younge, *A Christian Library* (1655). For statistics on New England clergy who published, see

George Selement, "Publication and the Puritan Minister," *William and Mary Quarterly* 37 (1980). Using a different criterion for identifying his subjects, Selement finds that fewer than one-third of the first-generation clergy published anything.

12.   John Preston quoted in Sargent Bush, Jr., "Hearing the Word as Spoken," *Early American Literature* 22 (1987): 138. George Selement in "Publication" points to some authors of printed sermons who dismissed their work as hastily composed. While it is difficult to be certain, I suspect that much of this attitude is authorial false modesty.

13.   Harry S. Stout, *The New England Soul* (New York, 1986), 35; Thomas Shepard, "Journal," in Michael McGiffert, ed., *God's Plot, The Paradoxes of Puritan Piety: Being the Autobiography and Journal of Thomas Shepard* (Amherst, Mass., 1972), 85.

14.   Richard Baxter to Abraham Pinchbecke, 5 July 1654, *Calendar 1*, 146–48. Though Baxter was not a New Englander, he was culturally part of the transatlantic Puritan community that included the New Englanders. He was a moderate Presbyterian and became suspected of holding Arminian tendencies, in part because he was not very skilled at theologizing. His practical theology, however, was applauded by Puritans on both sides of the Atlantic, and he thought highly of the practical divinity of Hooker, Shepard, Eliot, and other New Englanders. He corresponded with a number of colonists in the midseventeenth century.

Chapter Three

1.   Thomas Allen, preface to John Cotton, *An Exposition upon the Thirteenth Chapter of Revelation* (London, 1655), hereafter cited in the text as *Revelation*; John Cotton, preface to Arthur Hildersham, *Lectures Upon the Fourth of John* (London, 1629).

2.   Lawrence A. Sasek, *The Literary Temper of the English Puritans* (Baton Rouge, La., 1961), 55, hereafter cited in the text; Charles Chauncy, *The Plain Doctrine of the Justification of Sinners* (London, 1659), sig A33.

3.   Cotton Mather, *Magnalia Christi Americana*, 2 vols. (London, 1702), 1:377, hereafter cited in the text as *Magnalia*.

4.   Thomas Hooker, *The Application of Redemption, First Eight Books* (London, 1656), 1:206–8, hereafter cited in the text as *Application*; Giles Firmin, *The Real Christian* (Boston, 1742), (London, 1640), xxxi.

5.   William Hooke, *New Englands Sense of Old Englands and Irelands Sorrowes* (London, 1645), reprinted in Samuel H. Emery, *The Ministry of Taunton*, 2 vols. (Boston, 1853), 1:116–17; Everett H. Emerson, ed., *Redemption: Three Sermons by Thomas Hooker* (Gainesville, Fla., 1956), 132–33; Thomas Hooker, *The Souls Implantation* (London, 1637), 182.

6.   Thomas Shepard, *The Parable of the Ten Virgins*, in *The Works of*

Thomas Shepard, 3 vols., ed. John Albro (Boston, 1853), 2:281, hereafter cited in the text as *Shepard Works*.

7. Thomas Shepard, *The Sound Believer* (London, 1645), 318, hereafter cited in the text as *Believer*. An excellent discussion of the pilgrimage theme in Puritan devotional writings, and in Shepard's *Sound Believer* in particular, is to be found in Charles Hambrick-Stowe, *The Practice of Piety* (Chapel Hill, N.C., 1980), chap. 3, hereafter cited in the text.

8. See Paul Whitfield White, *Theatre and Reformation: Protestantism, Patronage, and Playing in Tudor England* (Cambridge, Eng., 1993).

9. Richard Baxter, *The Reformed Pastor*, quoted in Horton Davies, *The Worship of the American Puritans* (New York, 1990), 79; Samuel Clarke, *The Marrow of Ecclesiastical History* (London, 1650), 851; Daniel Neal quoted in David Leverenz, *The Language of Puritan Feeling* (New Brunswick, N.J., 1980), 171; John Collins's conversion narrative in Edmund S. Morgan, *The Diary of Michael Wigglesworth* (New York, 1965), 108; Oliver Heywood, *The Life of John Angier*, Chetham Society, *Remains Historical and Literary*, ns, 97 (1937): 50; John Howe, *The Works of the Rev. John Howe*, 3 vols. (London, 1834), 6:493.

Chapter Four

1. Thomas Hooker, *The Pattern of Perfection* (London, 1640), 1, hereafter cited in the text as *Perfection*.

2. Thomas Shepard, *The First Principles of the Oracles of God* (London, 1648), in *Shepard Works*, 1:339, hereafter cited in the text as *First Principles*; William Ames, *The Marrow of Theology*, ed. and trans. John Eusden (Boston, 1968), 83, hereafter cited in the text.

3. John Norton, *The Answer to the Whole Set of Questions of . . . Mr William Apollonius*, trans. Douglas Horton (Cambridge, Mass., 1958), 6.

4. Peter Sterry quoted in Nabil I. Mater, "A Devotion to Jesus as Mother in Restoration Puritanism," *Journal of the United Reformed Church History Society* 4 (1989): 304–14. Mater treats this aspect of Puritan imagery, as does Amanda Porterfield in *Female Piety in Puritan New England* (New York, 1992).

5. John Cotton, *Milk for Babes* (London, 1646), reprinted in Everett Emerson, *John Cotton*, rev. ed. (Boston, 1990) (hereafter cited in the text), 97, hereafter cited in the text as *Milk*.

6. Thomas Hooker, *The Application of Redemption, Ninth and Tenth Books* (London, 1656), 302–3.

7. Thomas Hooker, *The Saints Dignity and Duty* (London, 1651), 157.

8. John Cotton, *Christ the Fountain of Life* (London, 1651), 41; hereafter cited in the text as *Fountain*.

9. Thomas Hooker, *The Poor Doubting Christian* (London, 1629), 171.

10. Thomas Hooker, *The Souls Effectual Calling to Christ* (London, 1637), 158, hereafter cited in the text as *Calling*; Samuel Whiting, *A Discourse of the*

Last Judgement (Cambridge, Mass., 1664), 102; John Cotton, *A Brief Exposition with Practical Observations Upon the Whole Book of Canticles* (London, 1655), 2, hereafter cited in the text as *Canticles*. See also Michael P. Winship, "Behold the Bridegroom Cometh!: Marital Imagery in Massachusetts Preaching, 1630–1730," *Early American Literature* 27 (1992): 170–84.

11.   John Davenport, *The Saint's Anchor-Hold, In All Storms and Tempests*, in *Salvation in New England*, ed. Phyllis Jones and Nicholas Jones (Austin, Tex., 1977), 148–49, hereafter cited in the text as *Anchor-Hold*.

12.   Charles Cohen, *God's Caress: The Psychology of Puritan Religious Experience* (New York, 1980), 13, hereafter cited in the text.

13.   Richard Baxter, quoted in Francis J. Bremer, *The Puritan Experiment, New England Society from Bradford to Edwards* (New York, 1976, 25.

14.   For the antinomian controversy, see K. B. Stoever, *"A Faire and Easie Way to Heaven"* (Middletown, Conn., 1978).

15.   For the Quakers, see Carla Pestana, *Quakers and Baptists in Colonial Massachusetts* (New York, 1991), hereafter cited in the text.

16.   Thomas Shepard, *Theses Sabbaticae* (London, 1649), 65. See also Winton Solberg, *Redeem the Time: The Puritan Sabbath in Early America* (Cambridge, Mass., 1977), esp. 153–57.

17.   Samuel Whiting, *Abraham's Humble Intercession for Sodom* (1666), 147.

18.   See Robert Daly, *God's Altar: The World and the Flesh in Puritan Poetry* (Berkeley, Calif., 1978).

19.   For a demonstration of the importance of Puritan practices of piety, see Hambrick-Stowe, *Practice of Piety*.

20.   See Margo Todd, "Puritan Self-Fashioning," in *Puritanism: Transatlantic Perspectives on a Seventeenth-Century Anglo-American Faith*, ed. Francis J. Bremer (Boston, 1993).

21.   Giles Firmin to Richard Baxter, 4 June 1656, in *Calendar 1*, 214; Firmin used the same example in his *Sober Reply to the Sober Answer of Reverend Mr. Cawdrey, to a Serious Question Propounded* (London, 1653), 53.

Chapter Five:

1.   See Raymond P. Stearns, *Congregationalism in the Dutch Netherlands* (Chicago, 1940); Keith Sprunger, *Dutch Puritanism* (Leiden, 1982); and Stephen Brachlow, *The Communion of Saints* (Oxford, 1988).

2.   Thomas Shepard and John Allen, *A Defence of the Answer . . . Against the Reply . . . by Mr. John Ball* (London, 1648), 1, hereafter cited in the text as *Defence*.

3.   Richard Mather to "Dear Brother" [c. 1644], manuscript in Mather Papers, box 1, folder 11, Massachusetts Historical Society. Mather's manuscript "A Plea for the Churches of Christ in New England" is in the collection of the Massachusetts Historical Society.

4. See Robert Paul, *The Assembly of the Lord* (Edinburgh, 1985), for the best discussion of the deliberations of the Westminster Assembly.

5. John Cotton, *The Pouring Out of the Seven Vials* (London, 1642), sig Bbb4, hereafter cited in the text as *Seven Vials*.

6. John Cotton, foreword to John Norton, *The Answer to Appolonius* (London, 1648), trans. Douglas Horton (Cambridge, Mass., 1958), 14, hereafter cited in the text as Cotton Foreword.

7. Williston Walker, ed., *Creeds and Platforms of Congregationalism* (Boston, 1960), 109.

8. A. G. Matthews, ed., *The Savoy Declaration of Faith and Order* (London, 1958), 35.

9. See Robert G. Pope, *The Half-Way Covenant* (Princeton, N.J., 1969).

10. For a recent perceptive analysis of both Baptists and Quakers in New England, see Pestana, *Quakers and Baptists*.

Chapter Six

1. See Theodore Bozeman, *To Live Ancient Lives* (Chapel Hill, N.C., 1988).

2. John Davenport, *A Royal Edict for Military Exercises* (London, 1629), 16–17, hereafter cited in the text as *Royal Edict*.

3. Richard Sibbes, *The Souls Conflict with it self* (London, 1635), in *The Complete Works of Richard Sibbes, D.D.*, 3 vols., ed. Alexander B. Grosart (Edinburgh, 1862), 1:lix.

4. Thomas Hooker, "The Church's Deliverances" [5 November 1626], in *Hooker Writings*, 67, 71, 76, 87, 90.

5. William Ames, preface to Paul Baynes, *The Diocesans Tryall* (London, 1621); William Wilkinson quoted in William Hunt, *The Puritan Moment: The Coming of Revolution in an English County* (Cambridge, Mass., 1983), 87; John Cotton, "A Short Discourse . . . touching the time when the Lords day beginneth," in Winton Solberg, "John Cotton's Treatise on the Duration of the Lord's Day," *Sibley's Heirs, Publications of the Colonial Society of Massachusetts* 59 (1982): 521; Robert Baillie, *A Dissuasive from the Errors of the Time* (London, 1645), 80.

6. John Norton, *The Orthodox Evangelist* (London, 1654), "To the Christian Reader."

7. Thomas Shepard and John Allen, *A Treatise of Liturgies* (London, 1652), 3–5.

8. John Cotton, *A Brief Exposition with Practical Observations upon the Whole Book of Ecclesiastes* (London, 1654), 81, hereafter cited in the text as *Ecclesiastes*.

9. John Norton, *The Heart of New England Rent* (Cambridge, Mass., 1659), 30; William Hubbard, *The Happiness of a People* (Boston, 1676), 10.

10. Keith Stavely offers a perceptive discussion of the "unresolved, con-

voluted of the relationships . . . within the Puritan church and the Puritan state," which he sees reflected in Milton's depiction of the relationship between Adam and Eve, in *Puritan Legacies: "Paradise Lost" and the New England Tradition* (Ithaca, N.Y., 1987), chap. 2.

11. Daniel Rogers, *Matrimonial Honor* (London, 1642), 200; Thomas Hooker, *The Souls Exaltation* (London, 1638), 7; Thomas Shepard, *The Sincere Convert* (London, 1664), 171.

12. Thomas Hooker, *A Comment upon Christs Last Prayer* (London, 1656), 187.

13. [Thomas Welde], *New Englands First Fruits* (London, 1643), 12.

14. John Higginson, *The Cause of God, and His People in New England* (Cambridge, Mass., 1663), 6.

15. John Davenport, *A Sermon Preach'd at the Election of the Governor* (Cambridge, Mass., 1670), 4, hereafter cited in the text as *Election*.

16. John Cotton, "A Sermon on a Day of Publique Thanksgiving," reprinted in Francis J. Bremer, "In Defense of Regicide," *William and Mary Quarterly*, 3d. ser., 37 (1980): 103–24, 118, 121.

17. John Norton quoted in Stephen Foster, *Their Solitary Way* (New Haven, Conn., 1971), 72–73; "Thomas Shepard's Election Sermon," *New England Historic and Genealogical Register* 24 (1870): 366.

18. John Cotton quoted in Emerson, *Cotton*, 113.

19. William Perkins, *Treatise on Callings*, in *Perkins Works*, 1:727.

20. Patrick Collinson, "The Cohabitation of the Faithful with the Unfaithful," in *From Persecution to Toleration: The Glorious Revolution and Religion in England*, ed. Ole Peter Grell, Jonathan Israel, and Nicholas Tyacke (Oxford, 1991), 52–74.

Chapter Seven

1. Christopher Hill, *The Experience of Defeat: Milton and Some Contemporaries* (London, 1984), 307.

2. John Wilson, *A Seasonable Watch-Word unto Christians against the Dreams and Dreamers of This Generation* (Cambridge, Mass., 1677), 8.

Index

Allen, James, 92
Allen, John, 61–62, 76, 78, 93, 96
Allen, Thomas, 26, 96
Ames, William, 17–18, 22, 66, 78, 112;
    Medulla Theologica, 40–41
Anabaptists, 73
Andrewes, Lancelot, 7
Anti-Catholicism, 2–3, 5, 44
Anti-Synodalia Scripta Americana, 71
Antinomianism, 51, 52
Appollonius, William, 66
Arminians, 8, 44
Arminius, Jacob, 7
Ashe, Simeon, 61

Bachiler, Stephen, 95
Bale, John, 31
Ball, John, 61
Ballads, printed, 4
Baptism, 55, 70. *See also* Infant baptism
Baptists, 40, 72–74, 83, 102; Boston, 73;
    Particular vs. General, 72–73
Barrett, William, 7
Bastwick, William, 18
Baxter, Richard, 5, 23–24, 50, 70,
    126n14; on preaching, 21, 31; on
    printed word, 21, 22
Bay Psalm Book, 18, 55; revision, 55
Bayley, Lewis: *The Practice of Pietie*, 19
Bernard, Richard, 62
Beza, Theodorus, 3, 7, 44
Bible. *See* Religious literature; Scripture
Bible Commonwealths, 9
Bishop's Bible, 5
Book of Common Prayer, 54, 62
Bozeman, Theodore, 75
Bradstreet, Anne: *The Tenth Muse Lately
    Sprung Up in America*, 121
Bridge, William, 8
Bulkeley, Peter, 10, 12, 45, 46, 78, 96–97;
    Gospel Covenant, 51, 97; style, 29
Bullinger, Johann Heinrich, 3
Bunyan, John, 5, 73, 90, 92; *Pilgrim's
    Progress*, 30

Burr, Jonathan, 97
Burroughes, Jeremiah, 8
Burton, Henry, 18

Calvinism, 2, 3, 6–8, 15, 39; and Bibles,
    5; challenges to, 7, 39; and Lambeth
    Articles, 7; and salvation, 3, 7, 44. *See
    also* Predestination
Cambridge Platform, 66, 69, 109, 111
Canterbury, archbishops of, 8–9, 17
Cartwright, Thomas, 2, 59, 66
Catechism, 56–57
Cawdrey, Daniel, 69
Censorship, 17–18, 90; relaxation of, 20,
    21, 61
Chaderton, Lawrence, 56
Charles I, 9, 11, 76
Chauncy, Charles, 8, 27, 71, 73, 83, 89,
    97–98
Cheever, Ezekiel, 82, 98
Church of England, 2, 21
Clarendon Codes, 13, 19, 89
Clarke, Samuel, 31, 91
Cobbett, Thomas, 84, 98; on prayer, 54
Cohen, Charles, 48, 49
Collinson, Patrick, 3, 86
Congregationalism, 11, 58–60, 63–64,
    80; *Apologetical Narration*, 64;
    Dissenting Brethren, 63; vs.
    Presbyterianism, 12, 59, 63–70
Conversion, 44–45, 47, 49, 70
Cosin, John, 7, 9
Cotton, John, 2, 6, 10, 12, 16, 41, 66,
    99–100; and Anne Hutchinson, 51,
    99; *Bay Psalm Book*, 54–55; cate-
    chism, 43, 56; *The Churches
    Resurrection,* 79; code of laws, 85; and
    Congregationalism, 60; debate with
    Roger Williams, 68–69; on domestic
    relations, 81; education, 8, 99; *An
    Exposition upon the Thirteenth Chapter
    of Revelation,* 79; on grace, 48; and
    the individual, 49–50; *The Keys of the
    Kingdom,* 64, 67; on

Cotton, John (*cont.*)
  New England Way, 64; on Original
    Sin, 43; *The Pouring Out of the Seven
    Vials*, 32, 79; on prayer, 61; pub-
    lished works, 33, 39, 43, 79, 99–100;
    and Puritan Revolution, 63, 84; on
    removal to New England, 77, 78; on
    the Sabbath, 53; on sacraments, 55;
    scholarship, 22; sermons, 19, 20,
    26–27, 29, 32, 33–35, 37, 39, 45,
    47, 48, 79; on singing, 54; on society,
    80; *The Way of Life for God's Way and
    Course*, 39, 45, 50
Counter-Reformation, 1, 2
Covenant of Grace, 44, 49, 50
Cranmer, Thomas, 1
Cromwell, Oliver, 11–12, 69, 86, 106

Danforth, Samuel, 72
Davenport, John, 6, 8, 10, 12, 75, 76,
    78, 101–2; *Another Essay for
    Investigation of the Truth*, 71; biography
    of John Cotton, 92; and censorship,
    18, 20; on church government, 58,
    60, 61; on conversion, 66; election
    sermon, 33, 35–38, 72, 83–84;
    founding of New Haven colony, 9,
    11; on grace, 45; and Half-Way
    Covenant, 72; in Netherlands, 59, 60,
    101; published works, list of, 101;
    and Puritan Revolution, 63; on repen-
    tance, 93; *Saints Anchor-Hold*, 49, 91,
    92; sermons, 90, 94
Dod, Richard, 27
Domestic relations, 80–82; imagery of,
    29, 47–48, 81, 82
Dominion of New England, 12, 20
Dunster, Henry, 73, 82, 102
Dyer, Mary, 52

Eaton, Samuel, 89, 102
Education, 82–83; elementary, 82; of the
    ministry, 15–16
Edward VI, 1
Eliot, John, 8, 82, 89, 103; *Bay Psalm
    Book*, 55; *The Christian Commonwealth*,
    85, 90–91; *Harmony of the Gospels in

English*, 50; ministry to Native
    Americans, 87–88, 103; published
    works, list of, 103
Elizabeth I, 1, 13; Injunctions of 1559,
    17
Erastianism, 84
Espousal imagery, 46–48

Family devotions, 55–56
Fawkes, Guy, 2
Feoffees for Impropriation, 9, 101, 112
Field, John, 2
Firmin, Giles, 28, 56, 60, 89, 103–4;
    published works, list of, 104; *The Real
    Christian*, 60
First Bishops War, 11
Fiske, John, 105
Foxe, George, 52
Foxe, John, 1; *Actes and Monuments*, 5;
    Book of Martyrs, 5, 75
Free will, 7, 43
Friends, Society of. *See* Quakers

Gataker, Thomas, 21, 27
Geneva Bible, 5
God, attributes of, 41–42, 44
Goffe, William, 91
Goodwin, Thomas, 8, 32, 72; and
    Congregational movement, 58, 60,
    64, 66, 69; in the Netherlands, 10,
    78; *Patience and Its Perfect Work*, 92
Gorton, Samuel, 64, 67, 68, 73
Gouge, William: *Domestical Duties*, 81
Great Awakening, 94
Great Migration, 13, 78, 113
Greenham, Richard, 44
Grew, Obadiah, 19
Grindal, Edmund, 58
Gunpowder Plot, 2, 75, 76

Half-Way Covenant, 36, 70–72, 73, 80,
    101, 109
Hall, David, 20
Harvard College, 82, 97, 102; first grad-
    uate, 121; Indian College at, 87
Henry VIII, 1, 3, 17, 65
Herle, Charles, 65

Heywood, Oliver, 32, 125n7
Higginson, Francis, 89, 105, 116
Higginson, John, 71, 83
Hildersham, Arthur: *Lectures upon the Fourth of John*, 26
Hill, Christopher, 18, 89
Hobart, Peter, 63, 105–6
Hooke, William, 9–10, 28, 63, 89, 92, 106
Hooker, Thomas, 1, 2, 12, 14, 16, 42, 84, 106–8; *The Danger of Desertion*, 19, 40; on domestic relations, 81; education, 8, 106; and the individual, 49–50; on Lord's Prayer, 62; move to Connecticut, 9; in the Netherlands, 59, 60; and New England Way, 58, 65–66; *The Poor Doubting Christian*, 40, 56; on preaching, 28; published works, 40, 51, list of, 107–8; and Puritan Revolution, 63; sermons, 20, 31, 32, 39, 49, 51, 76–77; on sin, 43, 44, 46; on society 80; *Survey of the Sum of Church Discipline*, 65–66, 67; and uses of imagery, 30, 47–48, 49–50
Hubbard, William, 80, 92
Huit, Ephraim, 108
Hutchinson, Anne, 11, 40, 52, 67, 73, 99, 121; banishment of, 51, 118

Infant baptism, 55, 70, 72
James I, 8–9, 76
Jessey, Henry, 73
Johnson, Edward, 10
Julian of Norwich, 42

Keeble, N. H., 20
King Philip's War, 72, 88, 103
Knowles, John, 8, 108

Laud, William, 7, 9, 16–17, 18, 40, 114, 117
Leighton, Alexander, 18
Literacy, 1, 4, 5, 15, 27
Lollardy, 3
Lord's Supper, 55
Lothrop, John, 108

Marriage. *See* Domestic relations
Marshall, John, 8
Marshall, Stephen, 69
Mary Tudor, 1
Maternal love, 42
Mather, Cotton, 12, 27, 32, 57, 63, 93
Mather, Increase, 12, 16, 63, 72, 92
Mather, Nathaniel, 12, 71
Mather, Richard, 4, 63, 67, 71, 80, 89, 109–10; *Bay Psalm Book*, 55; on church government, 62, 65; on justification by faith, 44; "Plea for the Churches of Christ in New England," 62; published works, list of, 109
Mayhew, Thomas, 87
Miller, Perry: *The New England Mind*, 39
Milton, John, 90, 92
Mitchell, Jonathan, 72
Montagu, Richard, 9
Morton, Charles, 20, 92

Native Americans, 87–88, 114
Neal, Daniel, 31
Neile, Richard, 7, 9
New England Way, 11, 39, 63, 74; challenges to, 40; defense of, 64–69, 115; modification of (*See* Half-Way Covenant)
Newman, Samuel, 110
Norton, John, 8, 10, 12, 16, 22, 41, 78, 110; on conversion, 44; on an ordered society, 78; published works, list of, 110; on Quakerism, 52; *Responsio ad Totam Quaestionum*, 66; sermons, 92, 93
Noyes, James, 63–64, 111
Nye, Philip, 10, 58, 60, 64, 78

Oakes, Urian, 92
Original Sin, 42–43
Owen, John, 64, 69, 70, 72, 73

Paget, John, 20, 59, 101, 107
Parker, Thomas, 63, 111, 121
Partridge, Ralph, 111–12
Peck, Robert, 112
"Penny godly," 4

Perkins, William, 10, 15, 44, 56, 66, 77, 85; *The Arte of Prophesying*, 25; on domestic relations, 81; on preaching, 25, 26, 27–28, 31, 38; on predestination, 7

Peter, Hugh, 8, 9, 12, 58, 63, 112–13; execution of, 12, 89, 112; in the Netherlands, 18, 59, 60, 112

Phillips, George, 113

Phillips, John, 113

Pierson, Abraham, 113–14

Pilgrimage metaphor, 20

Plain style, 26–28, 32

Plimoth Plantation, 9, 59

Prayer, 54, 55

Predestination, 3, 7–8, 16, 39

Presbyterianism, 59; vs. Congregationalism, 12, 59, 63–70

Preston, John, 22

Printing, in Massachusetts, 18

Protestant Reformation, 1–5, 75; and print culture, 4–5

Protestantism: doctrines of, 27, 80; international, 1; ministry in, 14–16. *See also* Calvinism; Puritanism

Prynne, William, 18

Psalm singing, 54–55

Publishing: expansion of, 4–5, 15; licensing of, 17; in manuscript, 20–21; in printed form in New England, 21

Pulpit style, 31–38, 93–94; evangelical, 94; as theater, 31

Puritan conscience, 93

Puritan Revolution, 11, 58, 63, 83; and Restoration of 1660, 70, 84, 89

Puritanism, 2, 6, 8–13, 76–88, 90; at Cambridge University, 8; and church government, 58; and depictions of deity, 41, 42; and exodus from England, 9; factions in, 12, 39; and the Restoration, 12–13, 70, 89; and sacraments, 55, 71; tenets of, 14–15

Quakers, 14, 40, 52–53, 72, 83; executions of, 53

Rathband, William, 61, 62

Reformation. *See* Protestant Reformation

Religious literature, dissemination of, 4–5

Rhodes, John: *The Countrie Man's Comfort*, 4

Rogers, Daniel, 81

Rogers, Ezekiel, 57, 114

Rogers, John, 31, 32, 114, 115

Rogers, Nathaniel, 12, 27, 28, 110, 114

Roxbury Latin School, 82

Rutherford, Samuel, 65

Sasek, Lawrence, 27

Savoy Declaration of Faith and Order, 69–70, 106

Saybrook Platform, 70

Scripture, 5, 22, 27, 38; and deity, 41; focus on, 25–26, 30–31

Self-examination, 43, 49, 56

Separatists, 9, 59

Sermons, 33–38, 42, 51, 53–54; elements of, 26; imagery in, 28–29, 46–47; preparation for, 22–24; publication of, 18–22, 52. *See also* Pulpit style

Shepard, Thomas, 2, 6, 8, 12, 61, 78, 94, 114–15; on the deity, 40; and metaphor, 29, 30, 46; on prayer and psalm-singing, 54; published works, list of, 115; on sacraments, 55; sermons, 52, 85; on sin, 42, 46; *The Sincere Convert*, 56; *The Sound Believer*, 19, 30; *Theses Sabbaticae*, 53

Shepard, Thomas, Jr., 71

Sherman, John, 115–16

Sibbes, Richard, 47, 52, 76, 94, 101

Simile, use of, 28–29

Simpson, Sidrach, 8

Sin, 43; as excess, 50; and punishment, 44, 46

Skelton, Samuel, 8, 116

Society for Propagation of the Gospel in New England, 87

Spanish Armada, 2, 75

Spufford, Margaret, 4

Stationer's Company, 17

Sterry, Peter, 42
Stock, Richard, 27
Stone, Samuel, 12, 69, 116; sermons, 20,
    52
Stout, Harry, 23
Sunday services, 53–54
Supernaturalism, 5–6

Taylor, Edward, 23
Thirty Years War, 9, 11, 54, 76
Thomas, Keith: *Religion and the Decline of
    Magic*, 5
Todd, Margo, 56
Tompson, William, 65, 116–17
Trinitarian deity, 40
Typology, 29–30

Underdown, David, 86

Ward, Nathaniel, 63, 117
Ward, Samuel, 56
Warham, John, 117
Watt, Tessa, 4
Welde, Thomas, 8, 10, 62, 63, 68, 82,
    118
Westminster Assembly of Divines, 63;
    Confession of Faith, 66–67

Whalley, Edward, 91
Wheelwright, John, 8, 118–19; and
    Anne Hutchinson, 68, 118
Whitaker, William, 66
White, John, 86
Whitefield, George, 31, 32
Whitfield, Henry, 87, 119
Whitgift, John, 7
Whiting, Samuel, 54, 92, 98, 119
Wigglesworth, Michael, 41
Willard, Samuel, 92
Williams, Roger, 11, 40, 64, 120; debate
    with John Cotton, 68; *A Key into the
    Language of America*, 87; and
    Providence, Rhode Island, 120; pub-
    lished works, list of, 120; *Queries of the
    Highest Consideration*, 67
Wilson, John, 6, 32, 51, 87, 93, 120–21;
    education, 8; published works, list of,
    121; on Quakerism, 52, 121; *Song of
    Deliverance for the Lasting Remembrance
    of Gods Wonderful Works*, 2
Winslow, Edward, 67, 68
Winthrop, John, 6, 9, 13, 67, 75, 78, 79
Woodbridge, Benjamin, 121–22
Wycliffe, John, 65

Zwingli, Huldrych, 3

The Author

Francis J. Bremer is a professor of history at Millersville University of Pennsylvania. He is also the editor of the Winthrop Papers for the Massachusetts Historical Society. Dr. Bremer received his B.A. degree from Fordham College and his Ph.D. from Columbia University. He is the author of *The Puritan Experiment: New England Society from Bradford to Edwards* (1976), *Puritan Crisis: New England and the English Civil Wars, 1630–1670* (1989), *Congregational Communion: Clerical Friendship in the Anglo-American Puritan Community, 1610–1692* (1994), and numerous articles on English and American Puritanism. He has also edited *Puritan New England: Essays on Religion, Society and Culture* (1977), *Anne Hutchinson: Troubler of the Puritan Zion* (1980), and *Puritanism: Transatlantic Perspectives on a Seventeenth-Century Anglo-American Faith* (1993). He has organized major international conferences on transatlantic Puritanism at Thomas More College and at Millersville University, bringing together scholars in the fields of history and literature. Dr. Bremer has received fellowships from the Woodrow Wilson Foundation, the National Endowment for the Humanities, the American Council of Learned Societies, and the American Philosophical Society. In 1991–92 he was a Fulbright fellow at Wolfson College of Cambridge University in England. He is currently working on a biography of John Winthrop.

The Editor

Pattie Cowell received her Ph.D. from the University of Massachusetts at Amherst, in 1977. Her research has been directed by combined interests in early American literature and women's studies. She has published *Women Poets in Pre-Revolutionary America* (1981) and several related articles and notes on individual colonial women writers. Additionally, she has coedited (with Ann Stanford) *Critical Essays on Anne Bradstreet* (1983) and prepared a facsimile editon of Cotton Mather's *Ornaments for the Daughters of Zion* (1978). She is currently at work on a second editon of *Women Poets in Pre-Revolutionary America* and on a cultural study of early New England women poets. She chairs the English Department at Colorado State University.